IKEBANA

Ikebana

A guide to Japanese Flower Arrangement

Linda M. Walker

John Bartholomew and Son Ltd,
Edinburgh

© Linda Walker 1972
First published in Great Britain 1972
by John Bartholomew and Son Ltd,
12 Duncan Street, Edinburgh EH9 1TA

0-85152-900-3

Printed in Great Britain by
Bristol Typesetting Co. Ltd.,
Barton Manor, St. Philips, Bristol

Contents

For Wendy

Acknowledgements

My thanks to my parents for their encouragement and help and to my friends for free access to their gardens. Most particularly, my thanks go to my husband for his time and patience in taking so many photographs for this book.

CHAPTER I

LIVING FLOWERS

IKEBANA in translation means ' living flowers '. Gradually, over the centuries which span its development, this has come to be interpreted as ' the arrangement of material of a natural type '. Stemming, as it does, from an ancient art the traditional and symbolic are the basis for even the most modern Ikebana. The philosophy of the Buddhists, was, it is thought, the starting point for Ikebana and the Japanese love of nature and interest in the contemplative have played a great part in its development.

Records of floral offerings to the gods exist before the coming of Buddhism to Japan but flower decoration has been studied and practised as an art since the sixth century. It seems likely that the first real flower arrangements were those floral offerings made to Buddha in the temples, although they were not, at that time, known as Ikebana. So we see the origins of the art in the thoughtful, disciplined life of the Buddhist. It is rooted in the extreme simplicity of the Buddhist traditions and, although it has developed immensely, the early standards still apply today.

The Japanese people have a great love of nature and do not divide the growing of plants from the art of the flower arranger. The arranger is required to know his foliage and flowers and purists consider that you should

A*

be familiar with the growth habits and patterns of whatever material you use.

The first arrangements followed the style of the growing plant and although during the development of the art the stylised and formal have been the basis of the classical arrangements, still the character of the shrub, flower or other material has been retained.

Buddhism was brought to Japan from China sometime in the sixth century and with it came the builders of temples, the great bronze vases and the art of floral arrangement. The oldest flower school in Japan, the Ikenobo school, established the main principles of Ikebana in the eleventh century and by the fifteenth century the Rikka style was perfected. These large, often as much as fifteen feet tall, floral offerings to Buddha denoted life in terms of landscape and the pattern developed at this time is followed today although in a much freer and simpler manner.

Formal arrangements of this type were also to be found in the large households of court dignitaries whose servants would be very skilled in the art. They were, however, too large by far for an ordinary household and one of the Masters of the Ikenobo school formulated a new, simplified style which became the Seika arrangement more or less as it is known today.

As the art gradually came into general use the alcove, known as the tokonoma, became the centre for the offering to Buddha. Buddhist scrolls were displayed and a floral offering was made. Over many years the tokonoma evolved into a place where a few beautiful objects were displayed. The scroll might be a painting

Informal Rikka arrangement

or a fine piece of calligraphy, there would be a piece of bronze or a treasured ceramic and usually a flower arrangement or a small tree – a bonsai – elegantly placed.

Ikebana also became associated with the tea ceremony which came into being about the sixteenth century. Again the principles and rules were formal although the ceremony was designed to provide an oasis of spiritual comfort and pleasure to the participants. The simplicity of Ikebana was ideally suited to accompany the tea ceremony and became an important detail along with the carefully chosen and ritually used vessels.

Ikebana remained entirely a male province until the middle of the nineteenth century, indeed it is probable that no woman would have had the strength to deal with the large and complex Rikka arrangements. Eventually Ikebana began to be considered as a necessary feminine accomplishment and at this time, too, Japan began to be influenced by Western Ideas for the first time in its history. Fortunately the large schools held by the early principles and the purity of Ikebana was retained by the aesthetes.

Although the Seika and Nagiere styles had evolved some time before as a simplified form of the temple arrangement all arrangements were for upright containers. However, at the end of the nineteenth century the Moribana style emerged which utilised the top part of the formal Rikka style which was then arranged in a low container. From this many variations and free style arrangements developed, no doubt influenced by Western ideas, and Ikebana moved out of the tokonoma.

Seika arrangement

This, of course, opened up a whole new province because now the arrangement could be viewed from three sides whereas formerly it had been seen only from the front. More depth was needed and new materials used to fulfil the requirements of design. Fortunately the purity of the style harking back to the first rules and principles has been retained by the most reputable schools and, although they have developed and evolved, the styles have kept the harmony and beauty for which they were first created.

After the last war the Western world began to take a great interest in Ikebana and many Americans and Europeans became students of the traditional schools. Qualified teachers are now to be found all over the world and although they are trained in a variety of schools they all learn and pass on the underlying principles whether of the modern or classical schools.

For us it cannot have the significance that it holds for the Japanese but we can appreciate the long history of Ikebana and the continuing obedience shown to the early rules and principles laid down by the priests of Buddha. We can also appreciate the beauty of the arrangements, the careful use of materials to produce the designs of great simplicity which calls for knowledge, creative and artistic, of many different flowers and types of foliage.

Understanding of the delightful symbolism that runs through the styles and materials at our command will bring added interest and discrimination to our own designs and heighten our comprehension of the work of others.

Simple Nagiere arrangement

The great Rikka arrangements encompassed a whole landscape suggesting mountains, far and near, roads and rivers, the flowing movement of the wind and, even allowing for the sophistication of these arrangements, observation of nature and knowledge of plant material was essential. As in the past the teaching of Ikebana is based on the principles of plant growth and allied with this knowledge is the fascinating symbolism of the East.

The Japanese do not believe that one should only use perfect materials, the onset of autumn may be suggested by the inclusion of leaves that are past their best – perhaps torn by the action of the wind and rain. Nature is not perfect and to represent her properly we must take into account all her moods. The growth pattern of the individual plants should be faithfully adhered to in arrangements, indeed the style of the arrangement should be suggested to us by the form of the plant – the firm upstanding iris and the pliant stems of the broom show the need for the flexibility of arrangement within the same general framework.

Perfection in nature is denoted by the cherry blossom. However this is not always used in Japan for a happy occasion because the blossom falls quickly when cut which signifies death. Varieties of prunus in general symbolise purity, fidelity and truthfulness and peach blossom, a great favourite, represents feminine beauty and virtue and a happy marriage. Masculine perfection is shown by the iris which stands for male valour and purity, the leaves suggesting the sword of the samurai or warrior class.

The Lotus – in all probability used in the very earliest temple arrangements—signifies a noble spirit and sincerity of purpose. The lotus bud represents the future while the flower and the seed pod represent the present and the past respectively, in such an offering the whole of time was placed before Buddha. Long life and immortality are indicated by the use of pine and chrysanthemum while bamboo suggests resilience because the bamboo will bend before the wind and stand upright again when the storm is over. The paeony is much used to show prosperity and success and is particularly popular for arrangements that celebrate New Year when it will probably be combined with pine or possibly bamboo.

Ikebana requires observation of the seasonal cycle, spiralling material (willow may be so curved or wisteria vine may be naturally spiralled) will denote the seasonal round. Maple leaves with autumn colouring show the declining year while the camellia is valued for the crimson and white of its blooms which are the colours for a joyous occasion and stand for contentment—it appears in December and heralds the ending of the year. Care is always taken not to overlap seasonal materials. Many flowers can be bought out of season now but this is not considered a good thing as it is against nature. A spring design should be powerful yet simple representing the strength of early growth. Summer arrangements should have more material showing the availability of flowers in this season while autumn foliage and berries indicate the waning year and the winter arrangements are sparse and ' wintery ' in appearance.

Floral arrangement as it has developed in the West is a completely different art. Both Western arrangements and Ikebana use flowers and foliage, fixing methods, containers and accessories but in one thing they differ – Ikebana is not competitive. It is an expression of ideas and moods and with practise we are able to express overselves more clearly but it is never competitive and can only be assessed by a teacher trained in one of the recognised schools. An arrangement may be ' good ' or ' bad ' but not ' better than ' or ' not as good as '. Although the various schools have the same underlying principles Ikebana is always evolving and developing as the Flower Masters strive after new effects. Of late years some of the free styles have appeared to be far from the original precepts but the hard core of traditional arrangement is there, and having endured from the sixth century will continue to set the standard while the Westernised Ikebana will only enjoy a limited success before falling into disrepute. It would be a sad thing if the various styles of floral art were lost and we were left with a ' hotch-potch ' of ideas and half-remembered concepts.

Western flower arrangers have always favoured designs containing many blooms because in the West the material is more readily available. Sometimes a large number of flowers of one species is used and sometimes a multiplicity of species. Bunches of flowers gathered from cottage gardens – the ' tussie-mussie ' as it was called – would contain flowers of each species to be found in the garden on the day that the bunch was gathered. The great flower painters of Holland went

Free style arrangement

even further, they included flowers from all the seasons of the year in a single beautiful floral composition. From these early beginnings the Western floral arrangement has developed and from them also the lay man (or woman) can take courage. It is not necessary to use commercially produced perfect flowers to create the beautiful effects after which we strive. Watching the demonstration of floral art can be depressing as the expert produces great boxes of long-stemmed, thornless roses, enormous sheaves of gladioli and other, probably out-of-season, expensive blooms. But most of the really great flower arrangers of our time, starting with Gertrude Jekyll, have also been gardeners and from them we may learn the possibility of growing our own flowers.

For many of us the large arrangements are out of the question, we have neither the time nor the amount of material that we should require. So we turn to the Japanese style of arrangement which, in its simplest form, has an economy of material which is eminently practical. This economy was, initially, forced upon the Japanese by circumstances. The scarcity of agricultural land did not allow for the cultivation of flowers for decoration and so a flower or two would be combined with branches, bare or foliated, leaves, grasses and fruits to form the required arrangement.

The study of Ikebana means that we must discipline ourselves, no bad thing I feel, and also that we gather, grow and generally learn about our raw materials. It is a practical art. It uses practical materials and the use of natural material in a restrained manner calls forth all our ingenuity. I find the greatest pleasure in my arrangements when I have grown or gathered the material myself. I have never had as much pleasure from flowers – no matter how perfect that I have bought, as I once had from a few sprays of apple blossom from an old, forgotten orchard. The contrast of tiny green leaves and large pink-white buds gradually opening to show the yellow stamens, with the rough greyish brown branches was quite lovely. Before I had even heard of Ikebana I looked at my apple blossom and admired its simplicity and perfect interpretation of spring. So, for the gardeners among us who would take their art indoors and those who aspire to floral arrangement but must practise it on a budget, let us see what Ikebana can offer. An art which has come to us via India, China and Japan and which has endured for many centuries is worthy of investigation and study and we shall gain, in many ways, from both.

Camellias and Chaenomeles in a Nagiere container

CHAPTER 2

REQUIREMENTS

CERTAIN essential equipment is required for Ikebana but it is by no means necessary to rush out and buy specialised tools and containers before you may begin. Most of what you require initially will probably be found around the house or tool shed. Later, when you have acquired a little more experience, you can consider what else you need. It is very easy to start with a bang and buy all the items of equipment as set out in a manual only to find that many of these things are not initially required and that their purchase may well have been put off for some time. If, of course, you are able to join a class the advice of your teacher will be invaluable.

Containers, kenzan (pinholders), cutting tools and a few other items are the first essentials and even if you have never arranged a flower in your life it is probable that the only thing you will have to buy is the kenzan.

CONTAINERS

The essence of a container is in its suitability. Complete harmony must exist between the material forming the arrangement and the container. Colour and shape are important to the overall design and the material from which it is made must complement the material of the arrangement.

Strictly speaking, for Ikebana you will require two containers, a shallow, horizontal bowl for Moribana arrangements and a tall vase for Nagiere styles. This minimum will allow you to practise a variety of styles and learn to use your living material in conjunction with the various fixing techniques. If you are truly a beginner and have no collection of containers a look around the kitchen will produce the lid or shallow base of a rectangular or round casserole and a milk bottle or possibly a wine bottle that could be used for an upright container.

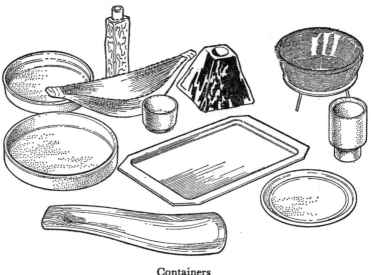

Containers

These suggestions may appear to be a very functional starting point for a work of art but using these very ordinary pieces of equipment you will be able to produce an arrangement whereas a more elaborate container could cause endless difficulties and fail to look right in spite of your efforts.

To begin with, at least, keep your containers as simple as possible. Neither the importance of the container nor the individual beauty of the flowers must be allowed to dominate and therefore destroy the overall design and unity of the arrangement. It is, in fact more important for the container to be a part of the design than for it to hold water. A well-kenzan will convert a shallow basket, of the type used for bread or rolls, into an eminently suitable container for a summer arrangement which is cool and airy in appearance. It is a delightful thought that in this instance, simplicity is firmly linked with economy.

Indeed there is no need for containers to be an expensive item. A collection may be built up gradually and meanwhile many objects around the home may be pressed into service. Most households acquire from somewhere those small trays which hardly hold sufficient china to serve as a tea or breakfast tray; lacquered in a suitable colour these would be ideal for Moribana or Morimono arrangements. Bath salts are often contained in attractively shaped bottles and I personally use a tall moulded-glass container which once held hand lotion. As you become more skilled in Ikebana you will begin to see possibilities in all sorts of unlikely articles.

A collection of containers can encompass china, pottery, glass, metal, basketware, wood and even vegetable matter in the form of gourds. When setting out to buy

a container consider the possibilities of metal, basketware and wood. Metal is particularly good as it has a
life-prolonging effect on plant material, basketware
and wood must be used in conjunction with a well-
kenzan or metal lining but each of these three materials
has the great advantage of being unbreakable.

China and pottery containers are perhaps the easiest
to obtain and some of the Japanese ceramics made
specifically for Ikebana are very lovely but, naturally
are rather expensive. Much of the china and pottery
now being made in Britain and America will be found
to have the simple lines required and a little time spent
walking round the china and kitchenware departments
will yield many examples of useful vessels – some of the
cooking utensils being imported from France, for instance, have delightful lines and good plain colours.

Visit your local potteries. Many small potteries are
producing well-designed pieces and colours and glazes
are improving all the time. If you are feeling affluent
the potter will probably be willing to make up something to your own design that is exactly what you want.
Most local authorities run evening courses for a reasonable sum and a little time spent at pottery classes will
give you great pleasure and also provide some interesting containers. Experiments in shape and simple texture
patterns with the application of different glazes will
produce containers which should blend very satisfactor-
ily with the natural materials used for Ikebana. Metal
forming is a rather more expensive business but is
equally rewarding. The materials are more costly but
the technique can be learned and a hand-made article

of this kind is so much more suitable than a cheap, poorly designed piece.

Some of the Japanese metal containers are very fine; bowls, trays, urns and moon-shaped containers are all made in bronze or copper. A sunabachi is an interesting type of container now rather rare but much used in Japan at one time. It was made in two pieces, the bowl was probably bronze and then a flat tray, of the same material fitted on top of this after the flowers were arranged, thus hiding the fixing method. Sand would then be sprinkled on the tray and the arrangement would take on the appearance of a landscape.

Bamboo was, and still is, much used for Ikebana as is wood. Containers of this kind usually have a separate vessel for holding the water so that the wood or bamboo is not spoiled by the water. Bamboo is often used to make the two-tier containers, called niju kiri, where the arrangement is on two levels. The same style of container can be made in pottery and is most attractive.

A variety of basketwork from all over the world is readily available now, and here again, it is possible to learn to make your own containers. The use of natural materials like wood, bamboo and basketry are particularly suitable for Ikebana because they have such an affinity with the materials of the arrangements.

Although it is not strictly necessary, a base is often used beneath the container. In some cases it is raised on legs or it may be simply a flat piece of wood, probable highly polished or lacquered, a rush mat or a ceramic tile. While not essential this does add a ' finish ' and has the added advantage of protecting the polished surface of a table with something that is in keeping with the arrangement.

Glass is not such a suitable container as many of the others mentioned, since water, unfortunately, tends to foul more quickly in glass containers. Plain glass is awkward from the point of view of concealing the bases of the stems and fixings while cut glass does not seem to be quite in keeping with the concept of Ikebana. Some of the modern glass that is now available is better, it has a more ' sculptured ' appearance and some pieces have geometric lines that are also very pleasing.

The seasons of the year are reflected in the choice of container as well as in the materials selected. The light and airy appearance of basketwork is considered suitable for summer arrangements, while metal is best used in the winter and ceramics for the spring and autumn.

Build up your collection gradually and remember that a good container will please as a part of the overall arrangement but will not distract the eye. The main points to consider are simplicity and suitability.

THE KENZAN

Kenzan is the Japanese name for the familiar pinholder upon which the materials for an arrangement are impaled. The weight of the base of the kenzan is important and where large or top heavy material is used a second kenzan may be inverted and the pins

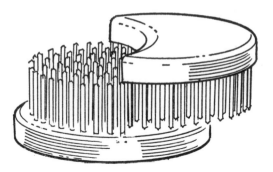

Moon kenzan used as a counter balance

locked into position on the first kenzan to supply a counter balance.

There are a variety of kenzans available, square, round or rectangular and these may be obtained in several sizes. It is usually recommended that a novice should start with a ' sun and moon ' kenzan. This is called a jitsu-getsu and consists of a round kenzan (the sun) and a three-quarter crescent from a circle of the same diameter (the moon) which fits against the round kenzan. These may be used as one, or the two sections may be used separately in a divided or combination arrangement. This type of kenzan is particularly useful when a counter balance is required and the flat base of the inverted crescent-kenzan may be used for the placement of tomi, or covering material, to disguise the kenzan. Tiny kenzans are used to anchor single flowers for Ukibana arrangements and kenzans with extra long pins can be obtained which will hold large, fleshy stems firmly.

A well-kenzan is a useful piece of equipment. This is

a combined pinholder and water container with a heavy
base. It is used where the main container will not hold
water as in the basketware containers or where part of
a large flat container may be used for a landscape arrangement and water is only needed for a small part

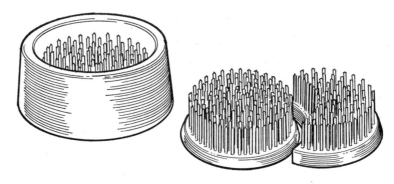

Sun, moon and well kenzan

of the scene. Dry material such as driftwood or bark
will spoil if left to stand in water and the use of a well-
kenzan will ensure its preservation while supplying
sufficient water for the live material.

Remember when buying a kenzan that the weight of
the base is very important. It is far better to start with
one or two kenzans of the right sort so that you may
learn to use them in the correct way. Inferior kenzans
will not have sufficient weight and the metal will probably rust, the kenzan must be strong and heavy because
you will want to impale tough, woody stems that would
bend weak pins or overbalance a light base.

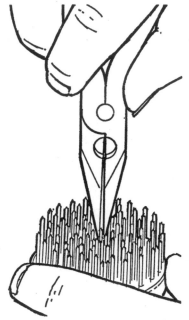

Straightening the pins

THE TOOL KIT

This is an important part of your equipment and special tool kits for Ikebana are available. However, it is quite possible to form a very useful set of tools similar to the kit recommended utilising many items which you may already have.

Cutting tools must be considered first. Scissors are not satisfactory but a good pair of secateurs will take the place of the Japanese ' hasami ' which are specifically designed for Ikebana. Any branch that is too thick to be cut with the secateurs will require a small saw. A sharp knife, possibly a pruning knife, is also useful. You will need something with which to straighten the pins of the kenzan, there is a special tool for this but I have found that a pair of sharp-nosed pliers will do the job – the ordinary sort are too thick and will not slip between the pins.

Spraying material to keep it fresh may be conveniently carried out with a syringe which, after removing its head can also be used for filling hollow plant stems with water. A wire cutter will be needed when lengths of wire are used for forming kubari or for lengthening a short stem and one or two different thicknesses of wire should be available; binding tape is also helpful where, for instance, groups of flowers and leaves must be bound together as with iris or narcissi. One or two rectangular pieces of wood six inches by eight inches and about half an inch thick, a small hammer and some one inch nails will assist with the fixing of heavy branches.

Keep your tools clean and in a usable condition and always try to arrange them in the same order so that you become accustomed to putting your hand out to pick up a certain tool from a certain place, this will avoid the frustration of searching around for the item that you require. I don't really recommend gloves for handling plant material, it dulls the sense of touch. However they may occasionally be necessary if handling thorny stems or, as I once saw at a demonstration, the finely curved but blackened stems of burnt gorse.

A few other items of equipment will be needed, a

Hydrangea and curving Broom foliage – Moribana

Free style table arrangement

Buddleia used for a boat at anchor

Mahonia leaves and *Chaenomeles Japonica* – Morimono

large piece of plastic sheet to cover the working surface will save time and trouble when clearing up, a tray is required to hold tools and fixing aids, plastic buckets are useful for holding plant material prior to arranging and a watering can will be necessary for filling up containers. I will cover the equipment used in the preparation of fresh and dried material in the appropriate chapter.

If it is possible to set aside a cupboard, or part of one, for the storage of your equipment you will reap the benefit of keeping it all in one place; much time can be wasted collecting equipment from several places each time it is required. It need not take up a great deal of space, the buckets will stack with the plasic sheeting folded inside. The trays will stand behind and the tools will not take much room if they are rolled in a cloth – the kits are sold in a specially designed case which is quite small when folded and fastened. I would advise having a few screw-topped jars to hold sand and small pebbles and space to store dried materials, stones, driftwood and so on. A shelf set aside for containers and kenzans more or less completes the requirement for storage space.

A useful time-saver is a list on the inside of the storage cupboard door which shows what containers you have, the dried material available and what you have in the way of stones or driftwood for tomi. Until I hit on this idea I wasted a considerable time going through the cupboard muttering to myself ' have I any birch bark? Did I keep those seed heads?' But now the list serves to refresh my memory and increases my efficiency.

B

For filling containers with water it is best to have a small watering can with a long spout. They are obtainable in metal or plastic and, although not so durable as metal, a plastic one will do very well. You can use a jug but it is so easy to disarrange something, the long spout of the watering can will keep you – and the body of the can – well out of the way while you fill up the container. Nagiere arrangements in particular need care when filling.

Work methodically from the start laying out all that you need each time you make an arrangement. In this way the mechanical part of the work takes care of itself after a while and you are free to concentrate on the creative aspect. Always keep one of your plastic buckets handy so that discarded material may be put into it at once, leaving your surface clear and tidy while you work. Plan your arrangement to suit a certain position rather than make an arrangement and then look for somewhere to put it. By following a disciplined pattern of work you will achieve the relaxation and serenity for which Ikebana is becoming known, worry or depression is pushed into the background while beauty and harmony is created. Each one of us has some measure of creative ability and it is delightful to exercise it with the study of Ikebana.

Double Nagiere arrangement

CHAPTER 3

MATERIALS

THE variety of material that may be used for Ikebana is very wide and its collection a real joy to those of a ' squirrel' nature who always return from any outing with pockets, baskets, the car or any other receptacle full of this and that.

Flowers and foliage are necessities and it must be remembered that much may be gathered from the countryside. If the garden does not yield sufficiently large branches of foliage for your needs the surrounding countryside will surely do so. All that is required of us is that we cut rather than tear the foliage and, where possible, obtain permission. It may not be strictly necessary but it is a courtesy that should not be neglected.

Both the garden and the hedgerow will yield a rich harvest at all periods of the year. Flowers, foliage, bare branches, cones, seed heads, berries, lichen covered twigs, driftwood or pieces of root and branch from fallen trees – even the blackened but arresting stems left after a gorse fire – will all find a place. Stones, pebbles and coarse sand from the beds of streams, grasses and heads of oats, barley and wheat – often to be found in the hedgerow in the autumn – these things and many others will go to make up your collection. Trees, for instance, will be found to produce more than foliage for arrangements; some have particularly interesting branch forms or colours – like the dogwood with its red stems in winter, while in the garden the *Leycesteria formosa* retains its vivid green stalks throughout the winter. Other trees and shrubs have flowers that are comparatively inconspicuous but which can be charming in the early spring before the leaves open and often nuts or seeds can be used at the end of the year.

Plant material can be used immediately or it can be dried and retained for later arrangements. Some material, like barley or angelica, will dry naturally and only require to be picked at the correct time of the year while other plants must be dried artificially in a warm atmosphere. Branches of foliage may be preserved by absorbing a solution of glycerine and water and thus provide sprays of beech or eucalyptus throughout the year.

COLLECTING

Collecting should be reasonably well organised if your plant material is to remain in good condition. Drift-wood, stones or any other heavy pieces, should be kept separate from the plant material to avoid damage. Take along a fair supply of large sheets of newspaper and some old dress boxes and treat each specimen with care. This applies equally to material which you intend to use at once or to that which you intend to dry or preserve, and it will ensure a quantity of useful material rather than a tangle of plant life that is spoiled as you strive to separate the stems.

Cut your chosen plants carefully and either lay them

out in a large box with sheets of newspaper separating
the layers or roll each specimen up in a separate sheet
so that the twigs and flowers don't tangle. Material that
is to be used fresh, I prefer to roll in newspaper and
then, immediately I get home, I place them all – still
rolled up – in buckets of water to revive and wait till
I have time to attend properly to conditioning the
material for use. It is surprising what a difference this
treatment makes, if for instance, you have been gather-
ing catkins in the spring; it is so disappointing to lose
the delicate yellow ' lambs tails ' as you endeavour to
disentangle the twigs. Try also to arrange your material
so that the lighter and more fragile stems are in the top
layer.

A collecting trip in the car is relatively easy to organ-
ise but if you are walking then beware!' It is better to
limit your collection to a few items rather than to collect
as much as you can carry and spoil half of it. Small
things like seedheads and beech masts can be wrapped
and placed in a basket but twigs and branches will be
more difficult and a little restraint will be rewarded by
more perfect specimens.

CONDITIONING

Fresh material should, ideally, be cut in the cool of
the day – morning or evening. Most flowers are best
cut when just opening, the time must be judged carefully for if they are cut too soon the flowers may not
open at all and if cut too late they will fall quickly.
Foliage also needs care; some varieties should not be cut

before they are fully developed or they will not absorb
water and will droop pathetically no matter what you
do, the tender tips of the beech are a case in point.

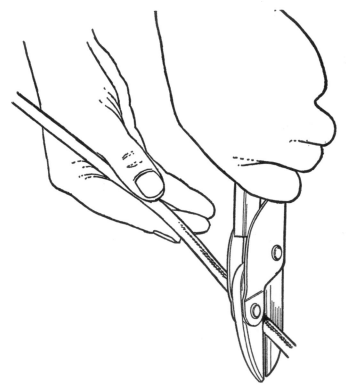

Cutting the stem at the correct angle

Branches of leaves will always benefit from total im-
mersion because moisture is absorbed through the
leaves. Branches of flowering shrubs should have some

or all of the leaves removed, since the amount of moisture given off is considerable, and the removal of some
of the leaves will prolong the life of the flowers.

Woody stems of shrubs or trees should be crushed for
the bottom inch or so to allow the water to be absorbed
more readily. Cut in the cool of the evening, treated as
described and left deeply immersed in a bucket of water
the branches will last very well indeed. Jointed stems –
pinks, for instance – should be cut between the joints
where the water is taken up more easily. Take care,
when cutting the end of a stem prior to making your
arrangement, that it is cut on a slant. If it is cut straight
across there is always the danger that the cut end will
be flush with the base of the container and the stem
will be unable to draw in the water. Hollow stems need
special treatment; after cutting, and before immersing
in deep water, turn the stems upside down and fill them
with water – do it gently so that no air is trapped –
then with a finger over the end of the stem, put it in the
bucket for a long drink. When cutting to the size required for the arrangement try to cut under water and
stuff the end with a tiny piece of cotton wool to keep
the stem full of water while arranging the material.

Almost all flowers benefit from having the stems cut
underwater, this treatment eliminates the possibility of
air bubbles preventing the water travelling up the stem.
Some plants exude slimy or milky sap when cut and this,
too, prevents the absorption of water, the condition may
be remedied by singeing the ends of the stems in a
flame or inserting them in boiling water for a short
while. This drives out the air in the stem and when it

Freesias depicting a 'full moon'

is placed in water the stem will take up water to replace the displaced air. When treating flowers in this way wrap them in a piece of cloth or towelling to prevent damage – it is only the bottom couple of inches of the stem that will require the treatment. There is another advantage obtained when this practice is adopted, the base of the stem is sterilised and bacteria will be slower to attack so that the life of the arrangement is prolonged.

If conditioning of material is delayed – as it might be if a gift of flowers has been cut for some time before you receive it – try to revive the flowers before conditioning. Spray the flowers and foliage gently all over holding the bunch upside down so that the water laden heads do not bend and snap, or immerse completely in water then wrap the bunch gently in damp newspaper for the whole of its length and leave it in a cool place to absorb water through the leaves and stems. After about an hour the material should be sufficiently revived to condition in the usual way.

Flowers grown from bulbs – tulips, narcissi etc. – do not require deep water in the container, the inch or so depth available in the moribana bowl is ample for their needs. It is not generally realised that the stems of these flowers absorb water only where they are green – the white portion at the base of the stem must be removed if they are to take in water. The slimy sap should be washed away before the flowers are put into deep water and, after a good drink, they will last well in the shallow water of the container. Tulips should be wrapped in paper before placing in the bucket so that the stems are kept straight while water is absorbed.

Some flowers, violets and hydrangeas come to mind, take in water through the petals and all arrangements will benefit if they can be removed from their positions and syringed liberally with a fine spray. The importance of fresh water must not be forgotten as this will help to check the development of bacteria. Stand the arrangement in a sink or outside and pour fresh water into the container until the stale water has been entirely replaced.

Occasionally plant material can be very difficult to keep looking fresh. There are several methods that you might try with more difficult subjects, some of which have long been used in Japan by the masters of Ikebana. The cut end of a stem can be dipped in salt – this will have the effect of increasing the absorption of water, it also helps to disinfect the stem and so deter the development of bacteria. Dipping the end of the stem into a little alcohol will have a similar effect and sometimes wilted flowers benefit if the stems are left in acetic acid or ordinary household vinegar for a minute or so. Try also, the effect of warm water – sometimes wilted flowers recut and left to stand in warm water will revive successfully.

PREPARATION OF MATERIAL

Although the fresh material has been gathered with an Ikebana arrangement in mind it is seldom possible to use such material in its natural state. This seems to be, at first, a contradiction of the importance of natural

forms and adherence to growth habits required for Ikebana. However, there is a difference in a large shrub
in leaf and a single branch of its foliage used in an
arrangement. For a natural effect the branch may require trimming and bending before it will be correctly
proportioned and suitably shaped for the arrangement
that you have in mind – it is seldom possible to find
exactly the shape and form required so what you
do must be suitably altered without, of course,
distorting the stems into unnatural lines. The rule
of simplicity will help when trimming material.

In the first place a branch with a great deal of foliage
will be out of proportion in an arrangement; secondly
it will give off more moisture by transpiration than a
sparsely foliated branch and so the appearance of the
arrangement and the length of its life are both improved
by judicious trimming. Also bear in mind the branch
itself so that damaged leaves or twigs are removed.
Symmetry of form is not particularly attractive and
material should be trimmed to avoid this and if ex-
cessive foliage is found on one side of the branch trim
it to obtain balance.

This all takes time to learn of course but gradually
you will find that you are able to look at an arrangement and say, ' I should have taken a leaf or two more
off it there ' – at first mistakes are easier to see on the
finished Ikebana. So, to begin with, trim off less than
you need and remove the remainder when the stems
are in place and the line and balance are clear. Ikebana
should be light and graceful and the line and style
evident.

The shape of the material at hand may need a little attention – again it is not always possible to obtain precisely what is required. Distortion must be avoided but the natural curve of a stem or branch often needs to be emphasised to produce the best effect. Do not try to curve a naturally straight stem – to attempt to bend bamboo would invite disaster and success (if it were possible) would be ludicrous. Some plants curve better than others and all bend more easily in the early part of the year when the sap is rising and the wood is pliant. The seasons must guide this process to some extent, at the end of the year the branches are brittle and will snap easily while the very new growth must also be treated with care as it is soft and sappy. Always bend with caution and to obtain a permanent curve twist a little as you bend, this will ensure that the branch does not straighten up when placed in water. Work gradually along the branch gently bending and twisting between the nodes (joints) until the desired curve is obtained. The Japanese are expert at this technique, they also use it when shaping bonsai which require the same instinct for balance and harmony as does Ikebana.

The larger branches may be too thick to bend in this way and for these there is the method of wedging. Decide where and how much you require the branch to bend and make a cut about one third of the thickness of the branch on the side which is to be convex. Open the cut and insert a wedge – previously taken from the end of the same branch – to produce the desired curve. The number of wedges needed is governed by the amount of curve required but they should not be closer than an inch or two apart. Cut sufficient wedges from the same branch to finish the curve so that the bark colour matches and the work is not noticeable.

If the branch is too thick to twist and bend but not thick enough for the wedging method try making a slanting cut on the underside of the branch – again about one-third of the thickness of the branch – and then twisting and bending; this should produce the

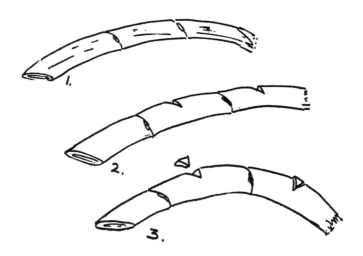

Curving by wedging
1. Curve to be emphasised   2. Cuts made between nodes
3. Wedges in position showing increased curve

necessary shape while still allowing the branch sufficient bark to draw up water without hindrance. Any marks left after the trimming and shaping operations may be rubbed with a little earth to disguise them. Some practise of these shaping techniques is necessary before you will produce professional results and when in doubt be guided by the growth habits and natural style of the plant.

DRIED AND PRESERVED MATERIAL

During the winter fresh material is not as readily available so it is as well to make provision for this time of famine by having a small selection of dried and preserved material to hand. Winter arrangements should reflect the season so that sparse, austere compositions are in keeping and dried material signifies the dying year. Most gardeners can supply a blossom or two during the winter months so it will probably not be necessary to rely on dried material to any great extent but there are a few items that are useful.

Wisteria vine provides curves and spirals and most years there are a few velvety green beans on the vine these will dry green if removed in time or, left in place, will harden and turn dark brown. Wild clematis – the ' old man's beard ' of the hedgerow – is beautiful when the seed head dries into a fluffy pompom. Various grasses dry well, Briza maxima (Great quaking grass) and barley are very effective ; gathered at different stages of ripeness they will provide a range of subtle colours.

Dried seeds can be very attractive, teazles, poppy heads, iris and honesty with its ' pennies ' are all very well known but try preserving instead of drying them and you will obtain new and interesting results. Seed heads for preserving should be gathered earlier than those required for drying as the preserving fluid must be taken right up into the material.

Study the form of the plant that you wish to dry so that the finished result is natural. Ferns, for instance, may be dried flat but other plant forms should be dried hanging upside down in small bunches, or singly where the stalks are thick and will take longer to dry, so that the stems are kept straight. There should be plenty of room for the air to circulate and a little warmth will help the process but remember that exposure to sunlight will spoil the colour of your material. The warmth of an attic where the plants can hang undisturbed is ideal. Some of the highly coloured foliage of autumn is worth drying. The leaves should be picked while the colour is at its best, and laid to dry on sheets of paper under the same conditions as the hanging bunches. These will prove useful 'tomi' for a dried arrangement.

When the material is thoroughly dry store it carefully in boxes. Florists boxes or dress boxes are suitable. You will probably not need a great deal of dried material but it is useful in winter and also for arrangements where it may be difficult to provide water for a fresh arrangement.

Preserved material is strong and long lasting and is much easier to handle than the somewhat brittle dried stems. Branches of beech and eucalyptus are preserved by standing, after cutting, in a solution of one part glycerine to two parts water. Oak, hornbeam and *mahonia aquifolium* leaves are equally suitable for this

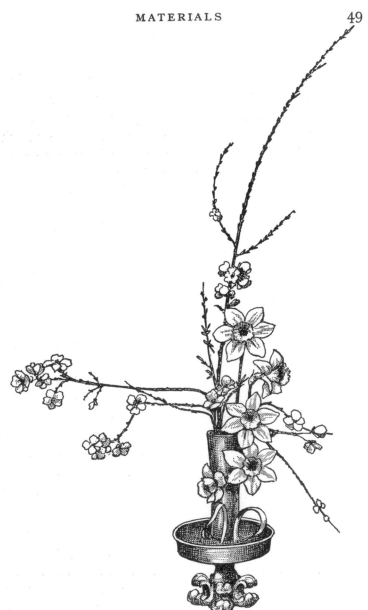

Narcissi and prunus in a Nagiere arrangement

method and although the material changes colour it remains pliant and is very durable.

When preserving plant material observe it carefully for the first day or so to be sure that the stems are taking up the solution. If the leaves appear to be wilting or withering slightly it may be necessary to re-cut the stems and warm the solution so that it may be taken up into the branch correctly. Some flowers could be tried, delphiniums and larkspur usually respond, and certain seed heads will preserve quite as successfully as they will dry. Decorative grasses are suitable and the fluffy pampas grass is much less messy when preserved.

Hydrangea heads are of great value and although technically dried they appear to have been preserved. The flowers should be picked as soon as they are fully out, they are then left to stand in an inch or so of water and as the water dries so will the flower heads; do not of course, leave them in the sun or you will lose the colour of the flowers. Experiment with drying and preserving because the various effects obtained can be a great asset to an arrangement. The natural shades of the dried or preserved material blend beautifully with fresh plants but a little care is required to ensure that the dried material is not spoiled by water. A well-kenzan used for the fresh material will overcome this difficulty.

When collecting, keep a look-out for pieces of weathered wood, drift wood, attractive bark, stones and pebbles of all sorts. Small stones and pebbles are useful tomi and often form part of the design – dark stones signify earth and white stones represent water when used in landscape arrangements. Look, too, for branches with an interesting shape for winter arrangements. Sometimes the bare branches are beautifully curved or twisted into unusual forms and will suggest the main line of an arrangement. Occasionally a branch will be worth retaining for its good line after it has been used in a spring or summer composition and the leaves are gone; it can be used as it is if the bark is good or this may be stripped away leaving a smooth, elegant shape.

A country walk or a stroll along the beach will usually bring some reward whatever the season of the year. As the lines and styles used in Ikebana become familiar the recognition of useful materials with good texture, colour and line will become easier and the scope of your arrangements will be correspondingly wider.

Scenic style arrangement

CHAPTER 4

BASIC IKEBANA STYLES

In Japan the Ikebana schools number more than two thousand and of these some twenty or so are major schools with large followings. Many of the larger schools now have accredited teachers living in various parts of the world.

Ikebana is considered by the Japanese to be an important part of a young woman's education. It fosters creativeness while teaching history, philosophy and discipline. She learns the symbolism surrounding the art and the nature of the materials required for its practice. Courses are quite long and twelve months might be the minimum as this is the time required to see the full cycle of the seasons and the materials available. The frequent exhibitions, not competitive in any way, draw large crowds of admirers. The styles of the various schools may be studied at these shows with a view to training with one of them. For our part we have far less choice of schools should we wish to learn the art in this country although here, too, we have some very good teachers of Ikebana.

All Ikebana has a common set of principles underlying its teaching, be it traditional or in the modern style. These fundamental principles are based on the growth pattern of plants. To understand this we should look at a large tree when it is bare of leaves. The pattern of growth is clear and if the tree is divided roughly into three, each section will be seen to have its own form.

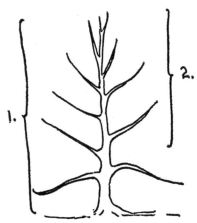

Pattern of growth upon which Ikebana is based
1. Seika   2. Moribana & Nagiere

The top portion grows upright with the branches only a short way out of the perpendicular; the middle portion shows the branches at a greater angle from the trunk while the third and lowest portion shows the branches horizontal or hanging with the tips only turning upwards. The classical Seika style is based on this shape and all styles are derived from some part of the ' tree '.

The simplest Ikebana styles are made up from three main stems and some supporting material. The three main stems may be called Shin, Soe and Tai and they symbolise Heaven, Man and Earth.

In any arrangement of any style Shin will be the longest Stem, Soe will be the medium stem and Tai the shortest of the three. These three elements may be used alone in the very simplest arrangements or the scope of the arrangement may be expanded by filling in with more material. Supporting stems are called jushis and must be of differing lengths, each one being shorter than the particular main stem which it supports.

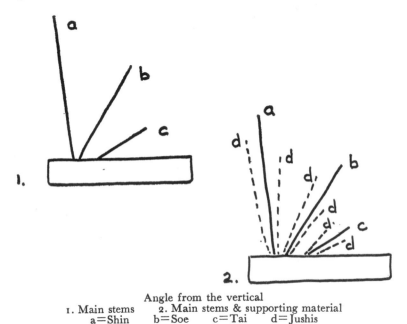

Angle from the vertical
1. Main stems   2. Main stems & supporting material
a=Shin   b=Soe   c=Tai   d=Jushis

Supporting material may repeat that used in the main stems but to retain the simplicity of the arrangement, which is the very spirit of Ikebana, not more than three different materials should be used in any one arrangement. It is possible to make the simplest arrangement using only one sort of material where the design is all important.

Whatever style of arrangement is used the nature of growing material must be borne in mind and the stems should appear to be growing from a common point as they would from the root of a complete plant. If a double arrangement is used there will be two common points from which the stems ' grow '.

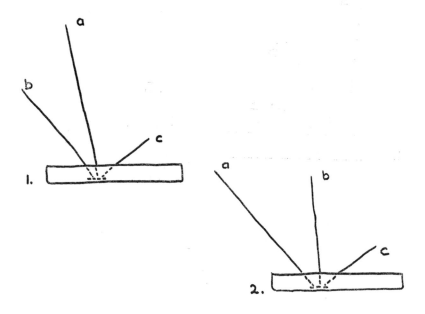

Variations on upright and slanting styles
1. Upright style   2. Slanting style
a=Shin   b=Soe   d=Tai

With the three stems, Shin Soe and Tai, a large variety of arrangements may be planned within the structure of the main styles. It is simply a question of the position of the longest stem or Shin. Once that is

decided the other two stems, Soe and Tai, are placed
in varying positions at a variety of angles from the
vertical.

To get a clearer picture of what is required go into
the garden and find a small shrub, a common azalea
will do very well, and look at it first from the side and
then from above. From the side the branches appear
to fan out and although we know that all the branches
are not on the same plane it is only when we look from
above that the number of directions taken by the growing branches is clear.

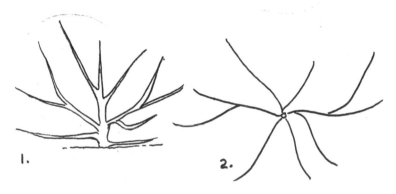

Directional slant
1. Elevation   2. Plan

Combining this directional slant and the angle from
the vertical — as shown by the tree — will produce the
correct structure, within which the three main stems
and the supporting material may be arranged. The
three main stems must each be at a different angle from
the upright.

To try this is really the only way to understand clearly

so take a kenzan and three stems, one long, one medium and one short and a straight stem to represent the vertical line. Place the straight stem in the centre of the kenzan so that it is perfectly upright, this will form the vertical.

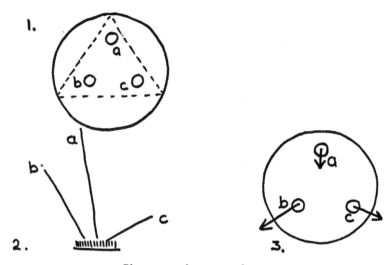

Placement of stems on kenzan
1. Position of main stems　　2. Angle from the oerlical
3. Directional slant
a=Shin　　b=Soe　　c=Tai

Now, the three main stems Shin, Soe and Tai must be positioned at three different angles – fifteen degrees, forty-five degrees and seventy-five degrees respectively – from the vertical and each slanting on a different plane. If an imaginary equilateral triangle is drawn on the kenzan each angle will accommodate a stem.

Shin is placed at the back at an angle of fifteen degrees from the vertical slanting a little towards the front.

Soe is placed to the left at an angle of forty-five degrees slanting forward and left.

Tai is placed to the right at an angle of seventy-five degrees slanting forward and right.

The three stems may change both their positions in the triangle and their angle from the vertical so, although at first the use of only three stems and three angles may appear very limiting, there are in fact a considerable number of variations which may be used.

When following the diagrams, which have been drawn 'flat' for simplicity, remember that each stem must take a different direction – the arrangement should not look like an open fan.

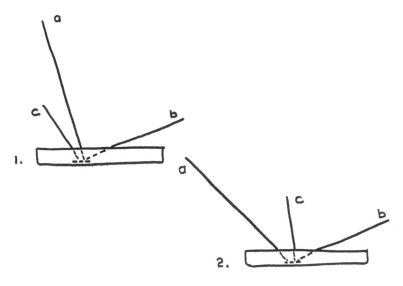

Variations on Upright and Slanting styles
1. Upright style   2. Slanting style
a = Shin   b = Soe   c = Tai

MORIBANA AND NAGIERE STYLES

Moribana, or low bowl arrangement, is the style most suitable for a beginner and with Nagiere, or tall vase arrangement, forms the basis of instruction in most schools. The methods of fixing are different and I will deal with these later but first we will look at the variations of style.

In the Moribana arrangement the stems may be arranged in either upright or slanting styles. The difference between these is in the angle from the vertical taken by Shin and Soe. In the upright style Shin is fifteen degrees from the vertical, Soe forty-five and Tai seventy-five. While in the slanting style the angles from

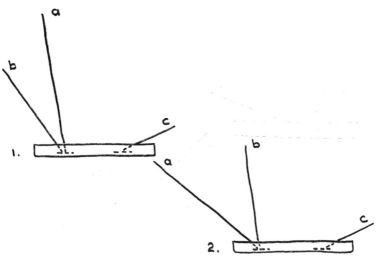

Double arrangement
1. Upright style   2. Slanting style
a=Shin   b=Soe   c=Tai

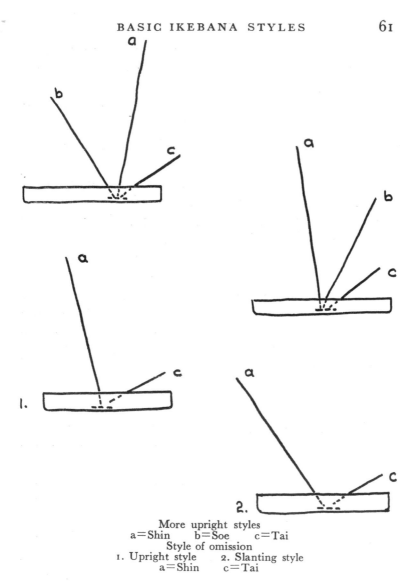

More upright styles
a=Shin   b=Soe   c=Tai
Style of omission
1. Upright style   2. Slanting style
a=Shin   c=Tai

the vertical of Shin and Soe are interchanged so that
Shin is at forty-five degrees, Soe is at fifteen degrees and

Tai remains at seventy-five degrees from the vertical.

Soe and Tai may also interchange in both the up-right and slanting arrangements.

Where a double arrangement is planned Shin and Soe will be in one kenzan and Tai in the other, each with its supporting material. Again, the arrangements may be in both the upright and slanting styles.

The diagrams show the styles in a Moribana container but any of the variations for Moribana will also be suitable for Nagiere, although the methods of fixing the material must, of necessity, differ.

There is also the ' style of omission '. In this case – often employed when arranging flowering shrubs – Soe, the medium stem, is not used. The arrangement consists of heaven and earth with man left out, I feel sure that this has symbolic significance to the Buddhist. The style of omission may be used in both upright and slanting styles.

SEIKA STYLES

The Seika style is a more formal arrangement. It came into being when the art of Ikebana became more general and began to be used as a decoration for the home. It was evolved from the formal Rikka style and follows the same principles although it is much simpler and suitable for the home rather than the temple.

Again we must illustrate this with the tree and this time the trunk must be taken into account. Traditionally the Seika arrangement must have a trunk above which are the three main stems. The formal interpretation of Seika is an upright style while the semi-formal and

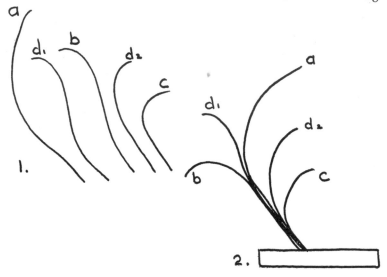

Seika style
1. Elements of arrangement 2. Composition of elements
a=Shin b=Soe c=Tai d=Supporting stems

informal styles are designed on more flowing lines. The trunk of the arrangement must be bare of foliage for about a handsbreadth above the container before it branches.

The Seika style may be arranged in an upright container or a low container and in each case the arrangements can vary in formality to suit the occasion, the material and the mood of the moment but in each case it is customary for the trunk to emerge from the container at an angle of forty-five degrees.

The large, very formal Rikka arrangements contain seven or nine main stems and a number of supporting stems but the simplest Seika style can be constructed with three main stems although supporting material is usually added so that there are five or seven stems. As with the Moribana and Nagiere styles the three main stems are long, medium and short and supporting materials must be between these in length.

The 'trunk' is formed so that the stems, whatever number is used, seem to be one. Above the trunk the stems must separate and curve outward so that a bird's eye view would show them pointing in various directions. Balance is achieved by bringing the tip of Shin curving back above the point where the trunk emerges from the container.

Seika arrangements can be made using only foliage or branches for the main stems and flowers may be used for the supporting material. This produces a delightful arrangement. Care should be taken to choose the main stems from material that will curve easily and naturally, willow or broom are suitable and aspidistra leaves are often used in Japan. Although the less formal Seika styles are arranged with flowing lines produced with curved branches and stems it must be remembered that all the arrangements are upright and even the most informal arrangements must indicate this.

The material may be held in place by a kenzan for the low bowl arrangement but for an upright container the kubari, or forked twig method, should be used.

LINE

Design is of great importance in Ikebana and one is constantly aware of the importance, too, of line. Material should curve naturally or be induced to do so

Free style Moribana arrangement

Maple and cherry-blossom – Nagiere

Spring arrangement – Moribana

Variegated leaves and seed heads – Moribana

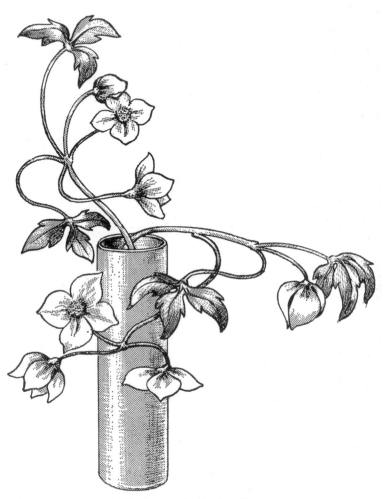

Nagiere with flowing lines

C

artificially so that a graceful line is achieved. Pruning away unwanted leaves and twigs to bring a good line into prominence is helpful, but where the material is naturally straight – for example the soldier-like stance of the iris – the line must be carefully preserved. There is great attraction in the contrast between the curves of willow and the straight lines of the iris where they are used in one arrangement.

It is essential that one is not led by the beauty of the flowers to make them the focal point of the composition. The beauty of each separate piece of material is incidental to the unity and harmony of the arrangement as a whole.

The line suggests the mood of the arrangement. The stiff verticals of iris leaves or wheat suggest strength and stability, movement is indicated by slanting or curving lines, the rhythm of the spiral shows the cycle of seasonal change – the eternal spiral of life. Particularly graceful are the descending lines formed by the growth of plants like clematis which are suited to Nagiere styles or to hanging arrangements. Contrasting a low bowl with a stiff, upright style or a tall, upright container with a flowing line is a delightful excercise in the art of design. Modern arrangements will sometimes rely on angular lines to present a harsh effect.

Lines drawn on paper produce shapes. The line of an Ikebana of any style should be studied and the forms and shapes enclosed appreciated as a part of the whole. Triangles, ovals, squares and circular shapes will be created unconsciously at first but by studying the effects produced they may be repeated at will as you become more expert. With these shapes it is possible to suggest moods of quiet contemplation or stark immobility, stability or the sharpness of change and great sensitivity can be expressed with the arrangements.

DIMENSIONS AND PROPORTIONS

The dimensions and proportions of the main stems and their relation to the container are important.

Let us first take the three main stems. The medium stem should be two-thirds of the length of the main stem and the shortest stem one-third of the length of the main stem. To discover the length of the longest stem, measure the width and depth of the container. A round, shallow container with a depth of two inches and a diameter of ten inches gives a stem length of twelve inches for the main stem. Depending on the arrangement, as much as half the length again may be added to this if desired so that the main stem could be from twelve to eighteen inches long. Whichever length is decided upon for the main stem of the arrangement the other two stems must be in the proportions given, if Shin is twelve inches Soe is eight inches and Tai is four inches.

The same rule holds good for the Nagiere style, in this case the height of the container may be ten inches and the diameter two inches so the main stem would again be twelve inches or up to eighteen inches. Remember, however, that the length of the stem is measured from the lip of the container and so sufficient length must be allowed to fix the stems in place.

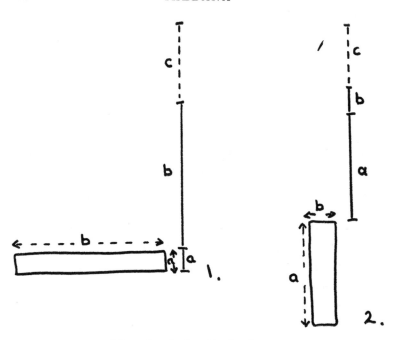

Measuring the length of main stem
1. Moribana   2. Nagiere
a=Height   b=Diameter   c=½ Diameter

Try to be accurate with the measurement of the stems right from the start. Take the longest stem and, tip down, measure the depth of the container from the bottom edge up and mark the point with your thumb on the left-hand side of the container, move your thumb back down the stem until it reaches the right-hand side of the container. When this point is reached you will have the basic measurement of the Shin stem. Soon you will find it possible to measure this with the eye and the proportion will almost always be correct but at first it pays to measure carefully so that your eye is trained to its work. Once you have the main stem length the others follow and are two thirds and one third of that length respectively.

If each main stem has two supporting stems each of these two must be shorter than the main stem in question and they must each be of different length. These proportions have been found to give the most harmonious and balanced arrangement.

Difficulties arise where the main stem length is not long enough. Little can be done in a Moribana arrangement but to select a fresh main stem. However with Nagiere, where a proportion of the stem is hidden, greater length may be obtained by inserting the end of the stem into a hollow stem or binding it to another piece of stem. When this is done care must be taken that the too-short stem is able to reach the water.

THE KENZAN — ITS POSITION AND USE

The Kenzan was developed in Japan and is the easiest method of making a really steady Moribana arrangement. With this invention came the possibility of a much wider variety of containers and the low bowl arrangements emerged.

There are various aspects to be considered in the use of the kenzan. In the first place the position of the holder in the container; this, of course, also applies if an open type holder or ' shippo ' is used. If a square container is used the kenzan may be placed towards any one of the four corners and using this as a guide we can place the kenzan in a variety of containers. The kenzan

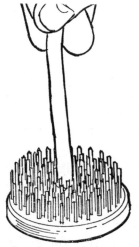

Impaling the stem on the kenzan   Stem slanted to required position

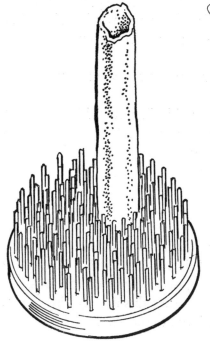

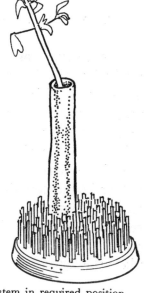

Support for thin stem   Thin stem in required position

would be placed in the centre of the bowl for a Seika arrangement.

The decision to place the kenzan towards the front or the back of the container is governed by the season. In the autumn and winter the kenzan is in the forward positions while in the spring and summer it is moved back and a cooling expanse of water is visible. Water is much admired in Japan both for its own beauty and for the beauty of reflected objects, it is used in a variety of ways in their pictures, gardens, bonsai and ikebana.

It requires a little practise to learn to use a kenzan. The sharp points will successfully hold the material firmly but it must be placed with care. Woody stems require a certain amount of force to position them and the stem should be cut at an angle the point of which is pushed between the pins at the chosen point, the stem may then be angled as required and thoroughly impaled so that it is firmly held. Delicate stems that cannot be impaled may be placed within a hollow stem which provides extra support. A stiff piece of stem may also be tied, like a splint, on to a soft stem to give it support. Where you have to resort to supporting a stem be sure that the end of the stem which is being supported is in the water and is not constricted, the water must have free passage.

Where a branch is very thick it is probably better to cut it straight across and then make two or three short slits up the stem. The end of the branch may then be impaled on several of the pins and be held firmly. Another type of stem which may cause difficulty is a hollow stem, dahlias are a case in point. In this case reverse the method used for a delicate stem; first impale a thin strong stem on the kenzan in the required position, the hollow stem can then be pushed on to the thinner stem and it will be correctly positioned and firmly held.

Where the inside of the container is smooth the equally smooth base of the kenzan will tend to slide out of position at the least pressure. A piece of paper or cotton material cut to the size of the base of the kenzan and placed between it and the container will prevent mishaps.

Kenzans of different shapes and sizes are used for different arrangements. The largest and heaviest kenzan will be used if the stems are heavy and require to be counterbalanced. Where this is the case position the kenzan so that the weight of the branch is to the left and the longest side of the kenzan runs from left to right then the longer length to the right will counter-balance the weight of the branch. If the branch is to be angled forwards place the kenzan so that the short side runs from left to right and the placing of a heavy branch at the back of the kenzan leaning towards the front will not cause it to tilt forward. When using the 'sun and moon' kenzan use the 'sun' for the heavier material to avoid the risk of disarrangement. More weight can be added to a kenzan by upending a smaller kenzan and wedging the pins on to the pins of the larger one, this provides a good counterbalance for extra weight.

METHODS OF FIXING FOR NAGIERE

There are, of course, a number of methods of fixing material. Possibly for a beginner they are not so easy as the kenzan but some knowledge of them is useful and essential for Nagiere arrangements in particular. It is possible to make an arrangement without a fixing device but this is mainly a matter of luck depending on the formation of the main branch and it is by no means reliable.

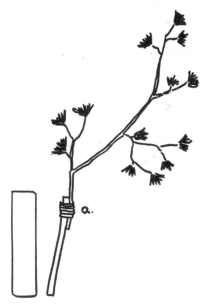

Nagiere stem lengthened at 'a'

The kenzan may still be used for a Nagiere arrangement if it is possible to position it in the container but do remember that it is heavy and if it falls to the

G*

bottom of an upright container while you are putting it in place a breakage may well occur. One method of using a kenzan to hold the main stem of a Nagiere arrangement is to take a short, stout piece of branch and impale one end on to the kenzan, the other end is slit and into this slit it is possible to wedge the main branch quite firmly in the desired position.

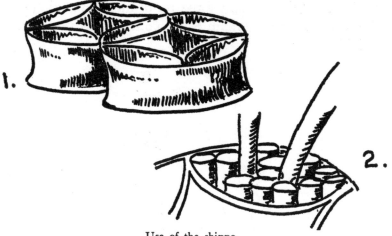

Use of the shippo
1. Shippo   2. Method of wedging stems in shippo

Some Japanese schools recommend wire for holding stems in place. This is a similar idea to the wire netting that is used for flower arrangements in the European style except that in Japan they use a length of plain wire and twist it into a mass of a suitable shape to fit into the container.

I have mentioned the shippo or open type holder that is used for Moribana arrangements. These are also called ' frogs '; they are heavy, like the kenzan, and are made of moulded lead. Some schools prefer to use the shippo because, unlike the kenzan, the base is open and there is less chance of the base of the stem being out of the water. When using a shippo thick stems are cut to fit the open sections of the holder and thin stems will be wedged into place with short pieces of material.

For Nagiere, however, the most usual method of fixing is by means of a kubari. Kubari are Y shaped twigs cut to fit the neck of the vase, the fit is improved when the kubari swells a little on contact with the water in the container.

Another piece of twig is cut to wedge in above the fork to hold the material in position. The forked kubari twig may also be used in a heavy metal ring, this obviates the necessity for wedging the kubari into the

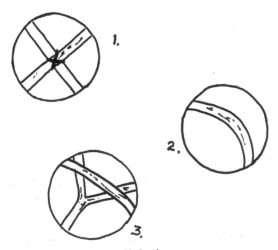

Kubari
1. Crossed twigs bound and fitted with container
2. Curved twig braced into container
3 Forked twig and crosspiece

neck of the container and possibly damaging a vase. The metal ring can be used for Moribana arrangements if a kenzan is not available.

It will require a certain amount of practice to fit the twigs into a ring or the top of a container. A forked twig may be cut and used as explained or a cross may be formed from two pieces of twig together. In either case cut it just a fraction longer than the ring or container requires; to put it in place tilt it and lower it into the vase. Bring it up and gradually straighten the twig ends against the sides of the container until it is firmly wedged. Care taken in cutting a kubari the correct size will save a lot of difficulty and frustration.

Sometimes a twig is curved and used in the neck of the container, the curve of the twig serves to brace it into position. A heavy stem can be slit at the end and a support twig inserted, it will probably need to be wired or tied into place. When the stem is arranged both ends of the twig will come into contact with the sides of the container and brace against it so that the stem is firmly held.

Nagiere arrangements may also be secured with sprigs of pine. Short sprigs are cut and pushed down into the container to form a network of pine needles into which the stems of the arrangement may be inserted. This method of fixing is made possible because of the much slower rate of decay of pine needles than that of other foliage. Lighter arrangements can be successfully positioned in this way but heavy branches are more stable if secured with the forked twig and bracing methods.

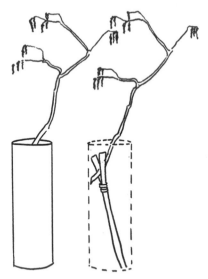

Slit stem support for Nagiere

Occasionally a very heavy branch is needed for a low bowl arrangement and none of the methods so far discussed will hold the material. In this event try the Japanese way, it sounds drastic but it is efficient. You will require a piece of wood about half an inch thick cut to a rectangle at least twice as large as the largest rectangular kenzan. Cut the branch to the length required for the stem it represents and, depending on the angle it is to take, cut it on the appropriate slant. Note the point on the board where the branch is to stand and turn the branch upside-down, drive a nail through the base of the board into the branch at the point selected – you will need assistance for this operation – and, when the branch is turned upright once more, it should be

firmly held in the position that you want. The board
with the branch attached is placed in the container and
the large kenzan is positioned on the board where it
both weights down the board and the attached branch
and provides a holder for the remainder of the material.

A Nagiere-style arrangement is able to keep its tech-
nicalities hidden in the tall container; a Moribana
arrangement must be helped by the use of Tomi. Tomi
is the Japanese word for the covering material used to
disguise the kenzan or other holder. Sometimes the
lower part of the arrangement itself will serve but where
this is not so material must be added. Tomi may consist of living material, large flat leaves or the trimmings
off the main branch, or natural material like stones or
driftwood. The choice of Tomi depends on the arrangement, the season and what is available. Where the
material to be used must be kept dry – as in the case
of drift wood – a second kenzan may be upturned and
wedged on to the pins of the stem holder and the re-
sulting flat surface will hold the drift wood clear of
the water (and must itself be covered of course).

A collection of stones and pieces of wood, roots, bark
and so forth provides a variety from which to choose
to suit different arrangements. River bed stones are excellent in conjunction with water – they have a natural
rounded appearance which is most suitable where an
expanse of water forms part of the arrangement. Beautiful stones are much prized in Japan, they are used in

the culture of miniature trees both for surface decoration and as containers – a large cavity holding the roots of the tree. The art of Suiseki is the portrayal of landscape by a stone, the contours suggesting hills, valleys and plains. Other stones represent flowers and are highly esteemed. Stone gardens are to be found in temples, the shingle between the stones being raked into patterns suggesting the movement of water and the whole designed to give a feeling of peace and preparation of the mind for contemplation.

Keep your Tomi in harmony with the arrangement and use only sufficient to hide the kenzan. Too much material will defeat the object, skilful choice and careful positioning is much more important and effective than merely covering the kenzan with a pile of miscellaneous bits and pieces.

Moribana – low container

CHAPTER 5

MORE IKEBANA STYLES

In the previous chapter we have looked at the basic styles, the dimensions and the techniques which are used for their formation. Beginners are well advised to restrict themselves to these basic arrangements until they become reasonably familiar with them and with the general principles underlying Ikebana.

The variations in this section still follow the basic principles but widen the scope for the arranger so that compositions can be arranged for a variety of situations and occasions.

FLAT AND HANGING STYLES

First I want to outline two rather more advanced variations of the slanting style, the flat style and the variations of the slanting style, the hanging style. The descriptions speak for themselves – the flat style slanting to such a degree that it is suitable for low situations and table arrangements and the hanging style looking well in Nagiere containers or wall containers where the material forms a graceful cascade.

The position for the main stem in the flat style is low, it follows, therefore, that with the longest stem in a low position the whole arrangement has a flatter appearance and is consequently more suited to viewing from above.

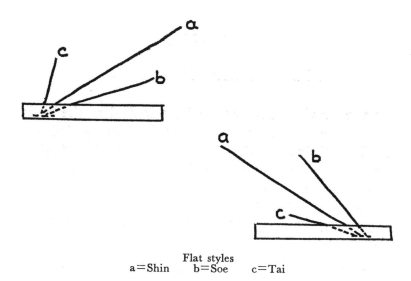

Flat styles
a=Shin   b=Soe   c=Tai

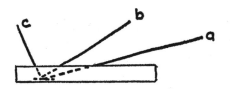

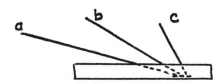

Flat style double arrangement
Flat style of double arrangement   Flat style of omission
a=Shin   b=Soe   c=Tai

When material is arranged in the upright style Shin is at an angle of fifteen degrees from the vertical, in the slanting style it is at an angle of forty-five degrees from the vertical while in the flat style the angle changes again and is between seventy-five and eighty-five degrees from the vertical. The medium and short stems can be at angles varying from ten to eighty-five degrees from the vertical.

Remember that these are only diagrams and that the stems take different directions as in the basic upright and slanting styles. This point is even more important when you consider that this type of arangement is often designed to be viewed from above. Care must be taken with the Jushi, or supporting material, that it does not disturb the flat appearance of the arrangement. Clearly too, particular attention must be paid to disguising the kenzan.

Shin is at a very low angle but do not let it touch the edge of the container – it is too easy to lose the air of lightness and delicacy that is the very spirit of Ikebana.

A double arrangement can be made using the divided kenzan as in the basic styles. The style of omission is also used, where the medium stem, Soe, is not included.

The hanging style overlaps a little with the flat style. In the flat style it is possible for the shortest stem to lie at an angle of one hundred and ten degrees from the vertical and unless this is placed in a Nagiere container it is obvious that the container must either hang or be situated on a high, narrow shelf to be seen to advantage.

The true hanging style is used only with a Nagiere

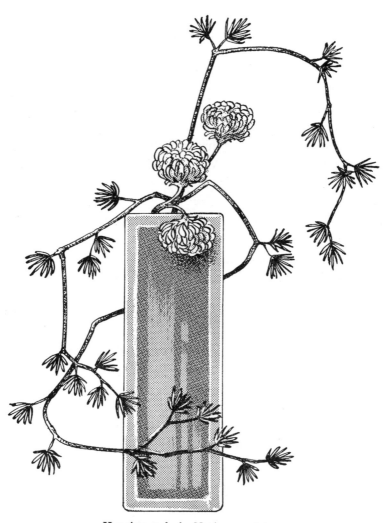

Hanging style in Nagiere container

container or a hanging vessel and for this the angle of Shin from the vertical is between one hundred and one hundred and twenty degrees. The other two main stems vary from fifteen to one hundred degrees in their angles from the vertical and can change both angle and direction whereas a change of direction only and not of angle is permissible with the Shin line.

Always match the ' degree ' of the hanging arrangement to the container – if all the stems have a downward flow the container should be particularly tall and graceful. Remember when using a tall container that the length of Shin is its visible length and that you must allow more for the amount that will be inside the container. The fixing techniques for the hanging styles in Nagiere containers are, of course, the same as for those in the upright and slanting Nagiere styles discussed in the previous chapter.

For any arrangements in the cascading styles be sure that the material is truly flowing in line and not just drooping over the side of the container. Take care also that the balance of mass and line is right so that the elegance of the flowing lines is accentuated by the focal point. The Jushis can either follow the flowing line or contrast with it and throw it into relief.

MOON ARRANGEMENTS

The moon in all its phases is dear to the heart of the Japanese. Its beauty is extolled in poetry throughout the ages and moon-viewing is a custom that has endured for centuries. Flower arrangements have long been made to accompany the moon festivals but perhaps the most interesting are those arranged in the very attractive ' moon ' containers. These may stand alone, be placed on a plinth or they may be hung in the desired position – this last being particularly suitable for the waxing and waning moons. The phases of the moon are represented by different arrangements and the seasons of the year suggest a great variety of material.

The moon container is usually made of metal and the kenzan is placed in the centre. All lines are forward leaning and therefore only one side of the container is used. The three phases of the moon are portrayed, the waxing moon, the full moon and the waning moon. To indicate the waxing moon the lines flow to the left, lines to the right show the waning moon while the full moon has the bulk of the material centrally placed.

The waxing moon brings the promise for the month and one of the classic materials used is wisteria. For the full moon white or yellow flowers are much favoured; yellow roses, lilies, hellebores and chrysanthemums are all suitable. Materials for the waning moon should be sparser and very delicate with soft colours and cascading lines. If the container stands on a table care should be taken that the cascading material does not touch the surface or the effect will be spoiled; the waning moon, in particular, looks well in a hanging container.

Work towards great simplicity in these arrangements, few flowers and little foliage is required but care in choice is important. Keep in mind the promise of the waxing moon, the pale beauty of the full moon and the delicate sadness of the waning moon.

UKIBANA, SHIKIBANA AND MORIMONO

These three styles are for use in a low position where they are seen from above. A low side table may be so decorated or they may be used as a centrepiece for a dining table, providing the beauty of an arrangement without the inconvenience of having to peer over it to see the other side of the table.

Ukibana is a Japanese term meaning ' floating flowers '. A shallow container, a plate or a tray, is used and the design allows a good deal of the water to show so that an impression of cool tranquillity is received. The container should be plain for preference to give an un-cluttered background. Black is good but a variety of colours are suitable providing care is taken with the choice of flowers and foliage.

The flowers used in such an arrangement must appear to float on the water and may be used with or without the stem depending entirely on the design. Tiny kenzans are available for fixing and will hold a single flower in place. Where the stem is required as a part of the design it must be bent to lie along the surface of the water. Do not attempt to bend into position without pinching it first or it will snap. Squeeze the stem firmly, with your thumb and forefinger, all round a short way below the flower head, the stem will then turn in any direction that you require and the short piece of stem immediately below the flower head may be impaled on the kenzan.

Where the flower head has no stem or too short a

Full moon arrangement

stem to allow the use of a kenzan it is possible to use
a little plasticine, shaped to support the head. I'm not
really happy with this idea however and now have
what I feel is a better solution. It is sometimes possible
to find a heavy ring, a finger ring or scarf ring, that is
ideal for holding a single flower. The fashion for large
rings has its uses!

Whichever method of support is used the flower
should be held just above the level of the water so that
it does not become waterlogged. Waterlilies are intended
to float on the water and are resistant to it until they
are at the end of their life. Flowers which tend to wilt
and droop in other arrangements are usually perfectly
suitable for Ukibana and will last much better in such
an arrangement. Hellebores, for instance, can be difficult to arrange but look charming when used in this
style. The measurement of the main stem should be
about three-quarters of the diameter of the container
and Soe and Tai in the usual proportion to Shin. The
angles of the stems used will be similar to those given for
the basic styles but are in plan rather than in elevation.
Take care to keep the water perfectly clear as it plays
an important part in the arrangement. No sign of the
fixing technique should be visible.

Shikibana is an arrangement without a container. The
flowers and foliage are arranged straight into the surface of the table and are ' spread flowers ' – the translation of the Japanese term. Flowers and foliage used in
this way are, of course, short term compositions; but
for some occasions it is preferable to having containers
and water on the table.

The size of the arrangement will be governed by the area available and the stem lengths are in the usual proportions. Although it is a short term arrangement the flowers and foliage will be required for some hours and must also be prevented from marking the surface upon which they are to be placed. Condition the flowers in the usual way and then, when you are ready to make the arrangement wrap the stems, first in a little damp cotton wool and then in oiled silk or polythene bound in place with cotton, so that the moisture is retained and there is less chance of damage to a polished surface. As far as possible choose material that will remain reasonably firm under these conditions. Ivy is a long lasting foliage and forms a good background for flowers and don't forget the use of berried shrubs for a winter arrangement, they are most effective against white damask or shining wood.

Morimono is a similar style to the previous two in the position that it occupies, primarily it is to be viewed from above and all its components are kept low. The container may be a flat basket, a tray, a piece of figured wood or a flat ceramic or glass piece.

The main lines of this arrangement should be composed of fruit or vegetables while flowers or grasses are used as Jushis. Fruit does not need to be exotic although grapes and peaches are beautiful used in this way. My own garden will provide materials like apples, chestnuts in their prickly cases, rose hips and so forth and decorative gourds will grow in any patch of ground or even a large flower pot. A spray of ripened blackberries and one or two autumn-coloured bramble leaves are always available in August and September. Glossy horse chestnuts will contrast well with autumn leaves and small bright chrysanthemums. Careful choice of colour is necessary for both material and container and where two similar objects are used care should be taken that they are not too regularly placed so that features like the stems face the identical direction thus appearing unnatural.

If the arrangement is wanted for more than an hour or so a well kenzan may be used for the flowers (it must be well hidden, of course). Basket-ware is rough enough in texture so that no other fixing is required to hold the components in position but if this is not the case try a heavy ring, as I have suggested with the Ukibana arrangements, or possibly a few pieces of twig arranged in a triangle – just to prevent the material rolling out of position. Sometimes a tight twist of vine, wisteria or clematis, can be used in this capacity.

Groom the materials so that fruit that should shine will do so and plums or other fruit with a " bloom " will not be marked and lose the natural beauty. Keep the seasons together in these designs to produce harmony; fruit and nuts with chrysanthemums or ears of wheat will suggest autumn, while summer arrangements may be made with bunches of currants – red, black or white – or a few cherries and any of the flowers and foliage abundant at this time.

A little thought will provide material for a Morimono arrangement at any season of the year – dried and preserved material helping out in the difficult days of winter and earliest spring.

DOUBLE ARRANGEMENTS

These very attractive compositions may be arranged in a single container or in two separate containers. Where a single container is used the material is arranged on two kenzans and each kenzan must hold a finished arrangement, each of which will harmonise with the other and between which there will be a connecting link. The same rule is followed where two containers are used, in this instance the containers may be both for Moribana or both for Nagiere styles or Moribana and Nagiere may be combined. Great care should be taken with combined arrangements so that they harmonise

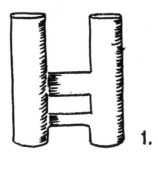

Double containers for
1. Nagiere   2. Moribana

and that the two arrangements are complementary to one another.

Interesting compound designs can be made in containers specifically devised for this purpose. The traditional Japanese bamboo is eminently suitable because of the nature of the plant itself which allows for arrangements to be placed at two levels. Many early containers were made of this material and modern copies are deservedly popular. Other contemporary containers are designed in ceramics and metal and may be found in a variety of combinations.

A double arrangement in a single container requires two kenzans or shippos and the larger group is traditionally placed toward the back of the container in summer and toward the front of the container in winter. This allows for a variety of landscape arrangements which can provide a great source of beauty and interest

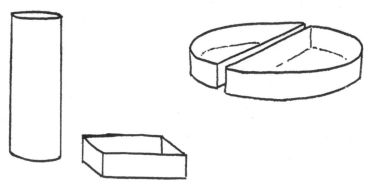

The placing of containers in double arrangements

throughout the year. Both water and land arrangements can be composed and besides flowers and foliage
there will be opportunities for using moss, stones and
interesting pieces of bark and wood, all of which will
help to create a small oasis of natural scenery.

Water arrangements are particularly effective during
the summer months giving an impression of cool, placid
waterside places. A composition of this style could consist of iris – the larger group having a bud for the tallest
stem. To keep the illusion of a pool the tomi used should
consist of small stones, smooth ones indicating the action
of water, or possibly water lily leaves. The iris flowers
and leaves should be combined in groups and bound together at the base before arranging as this is the natural
growth pattern. The groups are then arranged on the
two kenzans so that the finished work follows the principles of the Moribana arrangements.

A land composition of this style may be carried out
with narcissi or daffodils, the kenzan and the base of the
container being covered with moss to provide a green
' sward ', A layer of stones placed in the container beneath the moss would serve to lift it above the water so
that the flowers and foliage receive sufficient water
without saturating the moss.

Land and water arrangements may be combined most
pleasantly; moss forming the ' land ' at the base of one
part of the composition and edged with stone while the
second arrangement stands in the water. In a composition of this type the tallest stem is usually a branch so
that the effect is that of a tree at the edge of a pool or
stream. If the material is carefully conditioned such an

Bamboo container with two levels

arrangement can be made to last for some time by re-
placing flowering material as it fades.

Autumn and winter arrangements are best kept as
land compositions. Well kenzans may be used to hold
any living material which may then be combined with
dried and preserved material. A very shallow container
may be used or even a flat piece of wood, the two arrangements being linked by a drift of pebbles which
will also serve to cover the kenzans. These miniature
landscapes allow considerable scope for using ' collectors
pieces ' of twisted root, pleasingly shaped stones and
lichen-covered branches.

As I have mentioned before, early containers for
double arrangements were made of bamboo, some being
used vertically and some horizontally and both having
separate divisions for the two arrangements. These are
available today but now the same style of container is
also made in pottery or metal and some very modern
designs are on the market. The important thing is that
the style, the material and the container are in harmony.
Many interesting and original containers are made by
arrangers to suit their own ideas. The two openings of
the container may be at the same or at different levels.
Each opening bears a separate arrangement both of
which are carefully balanced and in sympathy.

Where the arrangements are one above the other,
as in the vertical bamboo stem, the lower arrangement
may be made to ' climb ' up to the one above or, using
the longer stems at the higher level, the arrangement
at the top may ' cascade ' down to meet that on the
lower level.

'Outward bound' boat arrangement

Magnolia and leaves – Moribana

Chabana – a single branch

The height of the double mouthed container governs the style of arrangement to be used. If the container is tall then a Nagiere style is called for, while a low container requires Moribana arrangements.

A double arrangement using two containers gives the opportunity of combining Nagiere and Moribana in one composition. Harmony must exist between the two sections so although the containers are of different heights they must be of a similar colour or material and the two arrangements must be complementary. The placing of the containers is also important and is dictated by the style in the taller vessel and the need for balance. When considering the dimensions remember that the main stem of the smaller arrangement should not be more than three-quarters of the length of the larger one. The same requirements of balance and harmony apply if two containers of the same height are to be used.

Another style of the double arrangement is the ' shadow ' arrangement. Two different Moribana styles are arranged in similar containers and one is placed directly behind the other becoming its ' shadow '. Each of the two arrangements may be made up of a different material so that they form a contrast.

Double arrangements have an infinite variety of possibilities although considerable skill and creative ability are needed to complete an harmonious whole from two separate compositions. Do not, however, allow yourself to be intimidated – all arrangements are formed with the basic styles and, by bearing in mind the principles and precepts laid down for these, the apparently difficult arrangements will gradually be simplified.

D

CHABANA

Chabana is the Japanese word for the flower arrangement gracing the Tea Ceremony. Tea was first brought
to Japan from China a couple of centuries after the
introduction of Buddhism and the formal, ritual ceremony of Chanoyu grew within the principles of this
religion. The ceremony is designed to form an interlude
of refreshing, peaceful simplicity ; it is very formal and
full of prescribed movements both of behaviour and for
the ritual of tea making. The host provides tranquil,
rustic surroundings, free from distraction in which he
may entertain his guests during the long ceremony. The
tea-house is situated so that guests pass through the
garden, the natural beauty of which is infinitely dear to
the heart of the Japanese. The guest, in his turn, is
soberly dressed, appreciative, respectful and humbly
admiring of all he sees. The atmosphere is that of restraint and understatement and the keynote that of simplicity.

A chabana arrangement must match the mood of
the tea-ceremony in its charm and simplicity. It should
be a natural arrangement and is, to a large extent, a
matter of inspiration. The composition should ' feel '
right in its choice of material and beauty of line. An
understanding of the principles of the tea-ceremony
itself rather than a set of rules guides the arranger so
that the chabana reflects the aesthetic harmony of the
occasion.

There are, however, certain precepts to be followed

if the arrangement is to be in keeping with the underlying Buddhist principles. Firstly it must be as natural
as possible, no shaping or bending should be required;
great care must be taken with the proportion of the
material to the container otherwise the tranquillity of
the arrangement will be lost. Very little material is
used and it must be chosen for the beauty of its line.
Any fixings should be entirely invisible and where it is
possible to arrange the stem or two used suitably, without technical aids the spirit of the chabana is sustained.

It is important that seasonable material be used in
the creation of chabana and that the container should
have graceful, uncluttered lines. Harsh colours and
jarring lines should be avoided in both material and
container. No material having thorns should ever be
chosen for a chabana arrangement as this would offend
against all principles of hospitality.

A chabana arrangement need not be confined to the
tea-ceremony, we, in the West, can use it to display a
particularly lovely flower or branch or to reflect a mood
of tranquillity and quiet, a small oasis of serenity in
the ' desert ' of our daily lives.

BOAT ARRANGEMENTS

Boat arrangements are amongst the most attractive,
expressing a variety of meanings. The ' outward-bound '
arrangement wishes well to the departing guest, the
' homeward-bound ' speaks of welcome. The ' boat-at-
anchor ' symbolises patience – the vessel will not leave
harbour until safe passage is possible. Supporting mater-

ial of a light nature and placed high in the composition signifies a swift passage, while heavier, lower jushis represent a prosperous and successful journey by suggesting a boat heavily laden with cargo. A suggestion of speed is produced with main lines of overstated curves implying that the sails are filled with wind.

Boat arrangement

The position of the arrangement used to be all important, they hung above eye-level in the tokonoma – in this position the water in the ' boat ' could not be seen and taken as an omen of bad luck. Later the arrangement was positioned according to whether the craft was homeward or outward bound. Where there is no tokonoma it is arranged so that the homeward-bound boat travels to the right and the outward-bound on the left. Only the ' boat-at-anchor ' rests on a base, the others have set sail from shore.

Choose a narrow boat-shaped container, it may be of any material – for example, basket work is often found in this shape and can be used in conjunction with a well-kenzan. The kenzan is placed in the centre and the curving lines lean to the bow of the boat to suggest movement. The graceful sails are tall so the main stem should be about twice the length of the container with the others in the usual proportion. Branches dipping over the edge of the container suggest oars; a single trailing stem in the ' boat-at-anchor ' indicates the anchor chair itself.

For the main lines of a boat under sail curving branches of leaves or flowering shrub may be used and for the furled sails of the ' boat-at-anchor ' iris, or some other material of a naturally upright habit is suitable. For the main lines of a swiftly sailing vessel use material that will bend easily so that the swelling ' sails ' can be shaped so that the curve of the main stem is almost over the bows and the tip of the stem is over the stern – the other stems following the same lines. The supporting stems represent the cargo and where foliage is used for the main lines the jushis may be made up of two or three flowers. These should be placed high up to indicate a lightweight ship or they may be darker and placed lower for the homeward-bound vessel.

FREE STYLE

Free style arrangements would, on the face of it, appear to present less difficulty – with regard to the set rules – than the basic styles and their variations. However, there is no doubt that the discipline of Ikebana must be learnt thoroughly before one is competent to launch

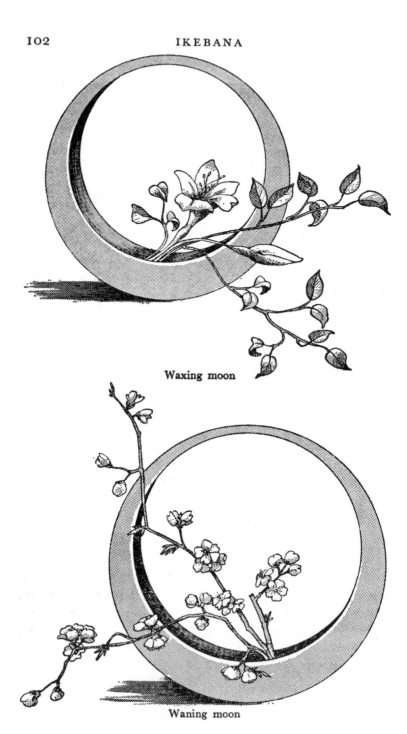

Waxing moon

Waning moon

into free style which has relatively few guiding principles. Within the confines of its discipline Ikebana
teaches balance and the movement of flowing lines,
in free style the rules are left behind but the harmony
created is a direct result of this teaching. To the carefully trained arranger an inartistic arrangement is immediately apparent. Jiyubana (free style) may be
realistic, so that a small scene of natural growth is
produced, or it may be abstract in design – relying on
form and colour for its impact. Again I must stress
that whichever style is attempted the artistic merit of
the arrangement is of great importance.

The growth of interest in free style is comparatively
recent and the style is still evolving so that many hitherto unused materials are being introduced into arrangements. Unusual containers may be incorporated as an
important part of the arrangement rather than as an
unobtrusive element of the whole. Some of the modern
free style arrangements have a truly surrealist appearance and, as with surrealist paintings, are not everyones
' cup of tea '; they do present a very large pitfall for
the inexperienced and unwary.

The main Ikebana styles are based on the natural
arrangement of material although they follow the rules
of placement and dimension but the free style arrangements do not have such rigid disciplines. The principles
of design, shape, line, balance and harmony should still
be adhered to – without these the arrangement will be
a hotch-potch of material rather than a free-style composition. Free style is a true test of your creativity and
proficiency.

There is considerable scope in free style for the use of dried or preserved material with its interesting shapes and masses and striking contrasts of colour and texture. Design must be almost an instinct if your free-style work is to be successful. Lines may deliberately cross one another and upright lines curves and masses may all be used in the one arrangement and although symmetry is frowned upon in the basic styles the more modern free style allows its use.

Line is of great importance in free-style arrangements and without the practise given by the arrangement of the basic styles the arranger will be unable to produce the forms he requires. Knowledge of materials and how to shape and groom them and about all the knowledge of the nature of the material itself will point the way to the effects you wish to achieve to fulfil the design.

More material is usually allowable in free-style composition but here again the artistic sense must be at work to prevent an overcrowded arrangement, the lines and focal points must be clear. Let your material suggest the form of the arrangement contrasting angular lines with bold mass effects and curving lines of movement with static uprights. Remember that lines enclose space, the creation of which is necessary to avoid muddle and overcrowding, but that these outlines will be accented with focal points of colour.

Whatever material is chosen for the main lines of the design that material must be shown to be all important and the supporting material must be subordinate to it. If the main line is not sufficiently dominating re-examine the design to find the fault.

Late winter landscape style

D*

CHAPTER SIX

IKEBANA AND THE GARDEN

THERE are two ways of planning arrangements. You can say ' I want an arrangement of such and such a type ' and go and get the necessary material; or you can say ' I have this and this and a little of that, and work out an arrangement from there. When your material is largely gathered from the garden you have a fair idea of what is to be found at various seasons and can plan your arrangements or go and see what is available and work on it. Sometimes the difficult days, the cold of winter or the rain of late summer, will leave very little in the garden but with careful choice and thought-ful arrangement good effects can be produced and these will give immense satisfaction because of the difficulty at first encountered due to lack of material.

ARRANGING THE GARDEN

To all who truly love green and growing things the arts of gardening and flower arranging are comple-mentary. Sometimes the gardener becomes the flower arranger and sometimes the flower arranger – urged by necessity! – becomes the gardener. Ikebana is the ideal projection of the gardener's art because it enables the greatest use to be made of the smallest amount of material the year round. This, of course, has a double advantage; in your efforts to produce a constant flow of material for Ikebana you also build up an astonishingly varied and beautiful garden with flowers and foliage for all seasons.

For those with large gardens the stress laid upon the use of flowering shrubs and branches of foliage will point the way to relatively trouble free gardening. Bedding out is surely the most tedious of all garden work and, moreover, requires continued expenditure year after year. To plant, instead, shrubs valuable for both flower and foliage will, in the long run, cost considerably less and give increasing satisfaction as the plants become established. In both large and small gardens the shrubs may be supplemented with carefully chosen perennials so that a few good blooms of the herbaceous variety are available at each season.

Certain considerations must be taken into account when planning a garden where plants are required for flower arrangement. You must not, for instance, expect to plant this week and cut next. Try to leave shrubs to become well established before beginning to depend on them for cutting. Choose shrubs and perennials that will tolerate cutting, some take it unkindly while others seem to revel in being trimmed and try all the harder to produce a mass of flowers and foliage – presumably to make up for lost time.

The nature of each plant should be carefully ascertained so that it may be placed in the most suitable position. Disappointment is bound to result and time and money will be wasted if plants are rushed in without due consideration of likes and dislikes and growth habits and

– important this – size when fully mature. Consider also the use that may be made of shade cast by shrubs. Hellebores and lily-of-the-valley produce fine flowers with long stems when they are grown in shady conditions. Taller plants, like flowering trees, may be underplanted with bulbs; many of these are suitable for Ikebana and will come up year after year demanding no greater attention than to have the yellowing leaves left to die back after flowering. Naturalised bulbs increase readily and the use of a few in arrangements will not spoil the display in the garden.

Gradually, as your garden begins to take shape and mature, your flower arrangements will widen in scope and through the knowledge acquired while growing the materials they will become easier to compose. Working always within the framework of the Ikebana styles the nature of the material used will indicate the form of the arrangement so that the transition from garden to house is barely noticeable. The need for new plants in the garden will lead to planning so that gaps in the flowering seasons may be filled and ideas for arrangements will cause you to experiment with hitherto untried shrubs or perennials.

When planning a garden, with or without flower arrangements in mind, certain basic principles should be followed. The garden must be interesting; it must not be allowed to appear as a square or a rectangle, the lines should be broken up so that there appears to be ' more in this than meets the eye '. As the garden is shaped varying conditions for growth may be brought about; shelter from wind, light, shade, protection from the morning sun or exposure to early rays. Useful foliage for arrangements is found both on the shrubs and below them where ground covering plants may be established to eliminate weeds. The walls of the house will support climbing plants each of which has a preference for facing North, South, East or West. Where hedging is required beech makes a good wind break as it retains its leaves through the winter; it is also useful to preserve a few branches of beech leaves for arrangements and this may be done afresh each year when the hedge is trimmed. Many flowering shrubs will take kindly to cutting and can be used to form a division in the garden. Other shrubs are better left as specimens and can be used as focal points for different seasons of the year. Cutting in this case should be done with care so that the shrub is suitably shaped.

For myself, I try to avoid flower beds, they allow for the invasion of weeds unless they are regularly cleaned and I prefer to use ground covering plants which will also give me flowers and foliage to use in arrangements. The Japanese garden runs mainly to landscape and where possible this, adapted to our own needs, makes an easily cared for garden. If your garden has several natural levels try to make use of them in the design rather than level the whole garden and risk leaving some parts with insufficient topsoil for healthy growth of plants. If there are any trees on your property consider carefully before taking them down. They may well screen a poor view or provide shelter from wind and will often allow the growth of plants requiring the shade that they cast or the shelter that they give.

Although they are said to be greedy in a garden, deciduous trees return some of the goodness to the soil; use the fallen leaves as a mulch around the surrounding shrubs and plants, it will discourage weeds, retain moisture and, as the leaves rot into the ground, will nourish the area.

If your garden is very small there are suitable foliage shrubs and slow growing trees that will help to landscape it so that there are varying levels of interest. Many of these species are Japanese in origin and are used for just this purpose in their native land. A large garden, on the other hand, will benefit from groups of shrubs and massed perennials; in this way a more natural effect is achieved, single plants are lost in a large area so plant several of each type or leave room and bring on layers or cuttings to put in at a later date.

Foliage is an essential item in the flower arrangers garden and, where Ikebana is concerned, can be of greater importance than the small number of flowers required. The foliage of a growing plant is greater in bulk and longer lasting than the flower and so, to follow nature's way, the Ikebana arrangement has the balance weighed on the side of the foliage. Many plants have the advantage of being grown for both flower and foliage. Others will provide different colours of foliage at different seasons – acer and witch hazel leaves have beautiful autumn tints.

Foliage can be used fresh or it can be dried or preserved, like beech and eucalyptus, in glycerine and water. Preserved magnolia leaves are useful in the winter when a bold effect is required – for Tomi they are invaluable. Beautiful Ikebana arrangements can be made if the twigs of deciduous trees are used just as the foliage emerges from the buds. The dainty, bright green leaves of beech, oak, and (my yearly delight) horse-chestnut are most appealing. They last surprisingly well and an arrangement can be kept for some time if the flower material is carefully replaced from time to time. The size of these early leaves is proportionately better than that of the mature foliage and such an arrangement is the very essence of spring.

The beauty of the Camellia is much admired in Japan but compared to the foliage the flower is short lived. The glossy green leaves are delightful and the branches are often beautifully shaped. As, indeed, are sprays of rhododendron grown in the shade so that the curving branches terminate in flat rosettes of leaves which last well in water. Where it is necessary to remove the leaves to ensure longer lasting flowers, as with chrysanthe-mums, or where the foliage does not last well in water, rhododendron or camellia sprays can be substituted.

Interesting colour is to be found on the *Cotinus Coggygria* the leaves of which turn red, yellow and orange in the autumn and which are borne on graceful branches. Pine can be used to great effect and is very popular for Ikebana both for its decorative effect and for its symbolic significance.

Yew is a good foliage to mix with flowers, the colour is strong and the branches bend well; it is much used for classical arrangements. Another well-known foliage plant is the pittosporum with its pale green leaves and black twigs, the variety *P. Tobira* is an evergreen shrub

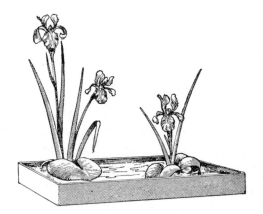

Water arrangement for summer

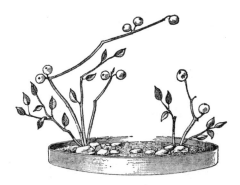

Land arrangement for winter

originating in China and Japan. Also from the East is the *Nandina sinensis* whose leaves colour to a beautiful red in the autumn. *Actinidia chinensis* is a climber producing large heart-shaped leaves which colour well towards the end of the year – this is a good tempered plant but one which requires plenty of room.

There are various species of eunonymous which are decorative but my favourite is the *E. alatus* with its ' winged ' twigs and bright red autumn leaves, fortunately it takes kindly to cutting. *Pieris forrestii* has the distinction that the new foliage is the most highly coloured and in the spring the new shoots are bright red with pink leaves.

I have tried to include in the following seasonal information plants and shrubs which will give the least trouble and which will best repay you, as a flower arranger, for the gardening that you do. For this reason I have left out the annuals although some of them are great favourites and may be considered well worth the extra work involved.

Of course in so large a country as the United States, the climate varies from region to region, and spring in Virginia begins quite a lot earlier than spring in New England, to mention only one difference. The reader will have to bear in mind the climatic peculiarities of his own area and reconcile the following suggestions for the growing of plants to the individual characteristics of his own locality.

Shrubs and herbaceous plants can be obtained to bloom at each season but the weather, colder or warmer than is usual, and conditions the previous year, a long mild autumn for example, can make a difference of many days in their development from one year to the next. Also by using the variations in the species a longer flowering period can be obtained, for instance the hellebores may be planted to give a succession of bloom from November to April. Snowdrops, also, have an extended season made possible by planting several species, there is even an autumn flowering species – *Galanthus corcyrensis*.

Where this method of extending the season is possible it is a good idea to plant the varieties together so that the garden is not ' chopped up' either in appearance or in the care that it requires. The leaves of snowdrops and other bulbs must be left to die back naturally and when they are naturalised this is easier to do if they have been planted in large clumps, that particular patch of grass may be left to grow until the leaves have yellowed off and then it may be cut as necessary again.

SPRING

I think it is merely that we are not so aware of the subtle changes of temperature as we might be but it seems to me that each year spring takes me by surprise. No matter how wet and miserable the weather may be the garden knows there must be an end to it and the buds fatten and leaves appear with great determination. A warm spell will bring things on a little faster but, incredibly, this may be followed by a cold spell which does not seem to hold things up at all. Clumps of snowdrops are followed by daffodils and grape hyacinths. The fat flower buds of the Japanese quince (*chaenomeles*) will cover the shrub with apple-like blossom in March (if the bull-finches haven't been there first!) and the willow, first silver and then gold with pollen, both wait to flower before the leaves appear. This type of shrub is particularly suited to the Ikebana arrangement. Witch hazel flowers on bare twigs make a splash of gold in the garden and later, in the autumn, the foliage is beautifully coloured. Bergenias will flower very early and the leaves are useful throughout the year, again changing colour in the winter. Even in the few plants that I have mentioned here there is a good variety of colour so that we do not become jaded with yellow and blue which some gardens tend to overdo in the early part of the year.

These early flowers really are like miracles; they appear to be so delicate but will withstand severe frost – indeed their lives seem to be prolonged by it, the cold doing less harm on the whole than wet windy days. Early flowering camellias are happier out of reach of the morning sun; after a frosty night they will brown immediately they are touched by the sun's rays, so a north wall and no early sun will give you unblemished blossoms amid the glossy green leaves.

I think that freedom from rough weather is a great blessing to the gardener. A good wind break can be formed with rhododendron, beech or yew which will provide both protection and a good supply of foliage all the year. It is worth noting that in the open rhododendrons will make a compact bush while under trees the growth will be more spreading and provide gracefully curved stems.

If you establish a plot for hellebores the Lenton rose, *H. orientalis*, is the one to plant for this season. It is not too easy as a cut flower but is worth a little extra trouble and if the stalks are put in about one inch of boiling water for a short while they should last well. *Cyclamen balearicum* will flower in March following the *C. coum* and *C. ibericum* of the earlier months. Each year as the spring progresses I watch the small bog garden beside the pool with some anxiety. A few years ago we established a couple of clumps of trollius there and each year the plants are producing more flowers; after cutting they need a long drink before arranging. A small boggy area near a pond will provide suitable conditions for a variety of useful flowers. Iris, several species of which require moist ground, are to be found to flower through the year and *I. siberica* is the first. The late spring will start the succession and at this time one may also find the yellow wild iris.

The anemones are spring flowers and the Caen and St. Brigid varieties are very bright and gay but I prefer the *A. plusatilla* or Pasque flower. This species is native to parts of this country and appreciates a little lime in the soil. It will usually do well near walls – I have seen them multiplying rapidly in the vicinity of south-facing stone walls and steps, probably getting sufficient lime from the mortar and delighting in the warmth of the sun. The delicate shades of lilac and pink are charming in spring arrangements.

Climbers are satisfactory plants for a small garden

– like skyscrapers in a town you get more plant for the ground space available. There are numerous kinds from which to choose and a succession of flower can be obtained from April to November. Clematis does well on a wall or it will ramble up a tree but try to put the root in a shady position – my own have their root run down under paving and do very well. There are a large number of varieties but the common clematis, *C. montana*, both pink and white are early. One of my pink clematis has been allowed to grow over a low wall and when in flower it looks for all the world like a pale pink eiderdown thrown over the wall.

Grape hyacinths are a fine bold splash of blue in early spring and, tied in bunches, are good for arrangements. Many bulbs are in bloom at this time of the year and if naturalised in grass they will come up year after year and look far happier than if regimented in borders. I have one patch of narcissi, planted in the sunny angle formed by two walls, which are in flower at the beginning of March and sometimes earlier, by planting in several positions the season can be extended considerably.

Forsythia heralds the start of the flowering shrubs and then there are so many it is difficult to know where to start. Azaleas, rhododendrons, chaenomeles and viburnums are all coming into bloom in March and April. Camellias too, sheltered from the morning sun, will provide flowers and foliage, I believe that Lady Clare, a fine pink camellia, is particularly good for cutting.

Japan is the country of cherry blossom and its people

plan great expeditions at blossom time to admire the trees. It is used in painting, embroidery and decorations of all kinds and for Ikebana too. Your selection for the garden will be dictated by the space available but even the smallest garden will accommodate the Poplar cherry – *P. amanagawa* – with its upright growth. Cherry blossom itself is rather shortlived but the winter flowering *P. subhirtella autumnalis rosea* will often continue to produce flowers through the winter and into the spring. This species is suitable for the small garden and is very good for cutting.

If you have a corner sheltered from the wind it is well worth planting a *Corylopsis pauciflora,* the pale yellow flowers are carried on attractively shaped branches. There are several varieties of Corylopsis if you should want to extend the season, some flowering in the winter months, but it is as well to remember that they are a little tender and need shelter – a good background of yew or rhododendron would provide both a wind-break and a good foil for the delicate racemes of blossom.

The flowering currant is a familiar sight in many gardens and a welcome one to the flower arranger. The most popular variety is probably *Ribes sanguineum* which grows vigorously, tolerates hard cutting and produces deep pink flowers in March and April. It can also be persuaded to work for you in the winter; cut several branches early, say in January, and leave them in deep water indoors – when they flower you will have beautiful sprays of white flowering currant for an arrangement. There are a number of other varieties but this one seems to be the best all-rounder, even used as hedging it will bloom freely and make a thick, well-clothed screen.

Sometimes it is necessary to give oneself a horticultural ' treat '. One of ours took the form of an eight foot specimen of *Magnolia soulangeana* for which we were charged very little, I feel sure the Nurseryman felt he could not charge a great deal as we were bound to lose so large a tree. However, working against all the rules instructing one to plant only young magnolias, we now have a beautiful tree coming into bloom in early April. To avoid disappointment position a magnolia where the early morning sun will not touch it – it has the same sad effect as upon the camelias. *Magnolia denudata* grows a little faster than other varieties and has the advantage that the flowers are borne on quite young plants. This magnolia is often seen blooming on North walls in late March and April, the bare branches accentuating the beauty of the flowers.

Wisteria vine takes on lovely curving shapes and, grown where its vigorous habit will do no harm, is an asset in any garden. Against the house it is beautiful when in bloom but unless ruthlessly trimmed it will cause trouble. Initial training and shaping must be followed by yearly pruning both to keep the plant within bounds and to encourage blossom. If the flower stems are dipped in oil-of-peppermint for a very few seconds the flowers, which tend to be shortlived, will last longer in an arrangement.

Late spring is the time for the azalea to come into its own. The Japanese evergreen azaleas flower very freely and a spray or two for an arrangement will not be missed. The deciduous azaleas do well in semi-shaded conditions and produce flowers on bare branches or as the leaves are opening. They are easy to propagate and generally easy to please, pick them when the flowers are nearly out and they will last quite well in water. Rhododendrons are coming out at the same time and many of these are suitable for arrangements although the smaller flowered varieties are the best. Even the humble *R. ponticum* has a good record as a cut flower and a surprising number of shades of colour are to be found in this common variety. The evergreen leaves are, of course, useful all the year round.

Lilac, now available in so many colours, comes into bloom in May the last month of spring. This is a shrub that is lime tolerant and one which will stand a sunny position. It is hardy and if suitably situated and reasonably well fed will provide considerable flower material. Fruit blossom comes in May and if you can spare just one spray of apple blossom you will be amply repaid, pick it in bud and watch it open in an arrangement.

Euphorbias – or you may know them as Spurges – are useful both for the foliage and for flowers, they will fill up difficult corners and help prevent the spread of weeds. The epimedeum is also a most obliging plant, it will do well in shade or in sun – I have some in the wood and some in the rockery – and is very hardy. The delicate flowers come in the spring and later the leaves colour charmingly, the mass of roots discourage weeds and makes it a good ground cover plant.

Paeonies come at the end of the spring season and

flower on into the early summer. These obliging plants can be obtained in both herbaceous and shrubby forms and it is a flower much beloved by the flower arrangers in Japan for whom it symbolises prosperity and success. Both forms require some shelter and both will tolerate shade; enrich the soil and don't disturb your paeonies and they will ' prosper and succeed '.

SUMMER

There should be no difficulty in finding flowers and foliage during the summer months, rather shall we find it puzzling to know just what to choose from the wealth of material available. Even so, early June can be rather a green period, the spring flowers being over and the early flowering shrubs covered with leaves.

Fortunately there are plants, like the paeony, which will bridge the gap. Certain species of rhododendron will flower at this season and one or two of these could be included where there is sufficient space. Many of the varieties that bloom at this time are very tough and welcome full sun and tolerate wind as the earlier varieties will not. Deutzias will also serve us well in June, there are a number of these, in shades of pink and white, which carry a profusion of flowers on lovely arching sprays. If they are cut just as the buds are breaking the sprays will last well in water. Either acid or alkaline soil is suitable and the shrubs will not object to light shade – a truly amiable inhabitant for the garden.

Leptospernums are not completely hardy but are very

good in milder districts. These finely leaved shrubs are evergreen and will produce a mass of tiny flowers in June. The variety Red Damask has double flowers of the appropriate colour while *L. flore pleno* carries double white blossom. Well drained, acid soil is the best coupled with a position in full sun.

Summer would not be complete without hydrangeas. There are many types and colours from which to choose but remember that the colour will be influenced by the soil in which they are grown. Alkaline soil tends to produce pinks and reds while blue is a more usual colour in acid conditions, white hydrangeas remain white in both types of soil. I particularly like the *H. petiolaris*, a climbing variety. It takes a little while to get started but once away will cover a wall or mount into a tree with enthusiasm. The foliage is most attractive in the spring when the leaves first appear and the flat corymbs of white flowers are out in early June. Later in the summer the Hortensia and Lacecap varieties are available, some being vigorous growers while others, like the *H. serratta* will remain quite compact and are suitable for the smaller garden.

Hydrangeas are very long lasting in the garden and sufficiently prolific to allow us to pick a few for drying for the winter as well as some for summer arrange-ments. A position in full sun is the most satisfactory, the plants may be affected by severe weather but they are hardy and will recover although the blossom may be less prolific if the plants have been frosted early in the year. Many of the finest hydrangeas come from China and Japan, a visit to a nursery specialising in hydrangeas will help you to select one or two good species for your purpose.

Roses begin flowering in June and continue for many months – into the winter even, if we have a mild autumn. Bush or standard roses are beautiful but unless grown in a carefully cultivated bed with considerable attention to pruning, feeding and spraying they will not give of their best. For the busy person who likes his plants to show a little self-reliance I would suggest the various climbing species. Unless picked in bud they do not last long in water but so many are produced that it is easy to replace one or two in an arrangement. I have two climbing roses (nameless as I received them as cuttings), a pink and a yellow, both are delicately scented and have the advantage of glossy, healthy foliage. Of course the flowering season can be prolonged if you can find the time to take off the dead flowers. Climbing or rambling roses are the thing to improve a dull tree or cover an old stump. I have in mind a tall conifer in a farmhouse garden which surprises the un-initiated by producing a mass of creamy roses each summer.

While we are on the subject of climbers it might be a good idea to include another clematis. There are a number of summer flowering varieties, such as Etoile Violette, whose graceful stems are of great value for hanging arrangements and for Nagiere.

A beautiful shrub for the garden is the *Cornus kousa*; although I have heard it described as delicate ours has given no cause for anxiety. It flowers in June and July, the sprays of foliage appearing to be covered with white butterflies. These ' flowers' are actually bracts which surround a group of tiny flowers, as the bracts mature they turn from a rather inconspicuous green to a beautiful creamy white. As a bonus the same shrub will provide finely coloured autumn foliage. Although I have called the *C. kousa* a shrub it is in reality a small tree, the shrubby cornus or dogwood is well represented by the *C. alba siberica* which is a delightful shrub with silver edges to the leaves and brilliant red bark.

Flowering at this time of the year but favoured more for its spring and autumn colouring is the evergreen shrub *Nandina domestica*. This plant, a member of the berberis family, is much used in Japan both in gardens and for flower arrangement. It is not very hardy and requires a sheltered position in the sun with a damp acid soil. If you can provide these conditions you will be rewarded with a variety of foliage colours through the seasons and a vivid display of red berries after the rather unimpressive flowers.

Of great interest to flower arrangers are the members of the lily family. For Ikebana they are used in conjunction with pine, camellia leaves and so on. There is an enormous variety in the lily family, and many of them are bulbous perennials and are reasonably hardy. Some require shade at the base of the stems and may be conveniently placed among low growing shrubs, azaleas for instance, so that the flowers have the benefit of the sun and the lower part of the plant is cool. Most lilies prefer an alkaline soil although *L. auratum* – the Japanese Lily – which is obtainable in white, yellow and crimson, and *L. giganteum* are happier in a peaty soil. Lilies resent disturbance but a dressing of well-decayed manure each spring will be appreciated. Most varieties bloom in July but careful choice will give you flowers from May to September adding much to the beauty of your garden and arrangements while causing little work after the initial preparation and planting.

Hostas are members of the lily group, they prefer an acid soil and are mainly plants for the shade where the leaves will be very fine. The flowers come better on plants that receive more sun but in such a position they will require more water. The large leaved varieties make excellent ground cover beneath shrubs and produce a range of coloured foliage for arrangements. *H. ventricosa* has dark green leaves while *H. glauca* has, as its name suggests, bluish foliage; the opened seed pods of this last named will last through the winter and furnish material for periods of flower shortage.

The well known Rose of Sharon also provides ground cover and blossoms freely but there are less 'rampageous' varieties in the form of good bushy shrubs which bear large buttercup-like flowers in July and August. *Hyperium patulum* Hidcote is a particularly good variety and *H. moserianum* is useful for the smaller garden.

In August the summer flowering shrubs and perennials are coming to the end of their season but the garden is not devoid of flowers because some plants have a very long flowering period and others, having bloomed early will now produce a second showing. *Jasminium officinale* is a deciduous climber with fragrant white flowers which appear in July and August. *J. o. major* is a newer variety with larger flowers but it doesn't bloom for so long a period as the original.

Fuschias are not really favourites of mine because most varieties are unco-operative in the garden. *F. Magellanica* is, however, reasonably hardy and it has several sub varieties which are equally so, one – *F. m. riccartonii* – can be used as a hedging plant. The flowers of these fuschias are smaller than the less hardy varieties but are charming for arrangements where the twisted branches contrast with the bright but dainty blossom. They require a well-drained position and should be planted low; in the autumn cover the crowns with peat or ashes so that if the frost is severe and some of the top growth is lost new shoots will appear when growth recommences.

Several Spiraeas bloom in the late summer, *S. bullata* and *S. japonica* and a hybrid of the latter *S. bumalda* Anthony Waterer which has stronger coloured flowers. Although I have included this genus in the late summer there are a large number of different spiraeas which will give a long season of blossom from March to August and September. These plants are easy to grow and have particular fads as to soil although acid soil tends to produce more vigorous growth; partial shade is acceptable and they last well when cut.

Late in August the winter daffodil flowers and a sunny position is the main requirement of this yellow crocus-like flower. They are said to be half hardy but in a good position they will grow and become established, *Sternbergia lutea* is the easiest to grow but if you add a few *S. clusiana* – which has larger flowers of the same

colour – the season of bloom will be extended. Light
soil and sufficient sun and warmth are the main requirements, it is worth a little trouble to secure the pleasure
of the flowers from late August until well into the
autumn.

AUTUMN

September heralds the autumn of the year. The days
are shortening and a nip is felt in the morning and
evening air. Often the fine, warm days of an Indian
Summer shortens our winter and encourages fine blossom the following year. A good autumn is worth a
great deal to the gardener, heavy dew refreshes the
plants and although the sun can be warm the ground
doesn't dry out as rapidly as in high summer. However,
we can also have the promise of winter with heavy
rains and high winds. Autumn flowers can be badly
damaged in such weather so where you can it is as
well to choose low growing varieties of perennials like
dahlias, michaelmas daisies and chrysanthemums.

When planning a trouble free garden it seems foolish
to include dahlias which require lifting and storing to
protect them from the frost, but they are excellent
flowers for cutting and, in this instance it may be
worth the trouble as they continue to flower until the
frost comes. It may be possible to leave them in the
ground if it is a well drained and reasonably sheltered
position; ashes or sand, heaped over the tubers after
the foliage has been cut down, may keep the main
enemies – frost and damp – at bay. There is an enormous number of dahlia varieties to to choose from and

it may be as well to consult an expert in the field for
advice as to the hardiest species. Short sturdy plants
require no staking and medium or small flowers are the
most suitable for Ikebana – although a large cactus
dahlia can be most effective in a modern free style
arrangement. Visits to horticultural shows are very
helpful when deciding which varieties you wish to grow
– enthusiasts are only too ready to talk about their particular subject and often give practical, down-to-earth
advice.

Michaelmas daisies are listed as hardy perennial
asters and they live up to that description admirably.
The flowering season is long and a variety of flower
sizes is obtainable with the colours ranging from white
through pink and red to blue and violet. The shorter
stemmed and dwarf vareties are good for edging shrub
borders and covering ground that is a nuisance to keep
free of weeds. These obliging plants have no particular
soil requirements and will thrive in sun or semi-shade
– although in this position they tend to grow a little
taller. For convenience they should be planted where
they can be left to increase undisturbed.

Chrysanthemums are another good autumn flower
but like the dahlia, they do require a little care. Probably the best variety for the flower arranger-cum-
gardener is the hardy Korean chrysanthemum which
has a good range of colours and some species not more
than eighteen inches tall. These can be planted in
clumps at the edge of shrub borders and to fill the
ground between shrubs or trees. Again I suggest con-
sulting an expert for advice because new strains are

Upright Moribana arrangement

leaves, it has a somewhat dry position in full sun and the effect in the autumn is striking.

Many shrubs give us fruits as well as foliage at this season. Chaenomeles carries its yellow fruits on bare branches in the autumn as it did its flowers in the spring, both are excellent for arrangements. A large number of the cotoneasters are evergreen and bear leaves and berries together, others are deciduous and the leaves change colour before they fall – *C. horizontalis* carries both red berries and dark red leaves for a while. These shrubs are wonderfully versatile and in both the evergreen and deciduous types you can find plants to clothe a wall, prune into a small tree or cover the ground; truly a gardener's boon and a flower arranger's joy in shape, leaf texture, colour, blossom and berry.

Enkianthus campanulatus gives bunches of small flowers, like harebells, of various colours in May and in the autumn the leaves turn red and yellow before they fall. All Enkianthus varieties require peaty soil which is not too dry in summer and some shade is appreciated. A useful shrub to grow in practically any soil is the Eunonymous, like the Cotoneaster, this genus produces a considerable variety of deciduous and evergreen species some of which are grown for their foliage and some for the fruits. Some of the forms are variegated while *E. alatus* has fascinating winged stems and leaves which turn pink and scarlet towards the end of the year. *E. japonicus* can be used as a hedge, it stands pruning very well. All are unfussy as to soil and the evergreen varieties will thrive in shade.

Leycesteria formosa will give pleasure all the year

with green, bamboo-like stems in winter, purple and white flowers in the summer and dark purple fruits in the autumn. Care is needed in handling the latter, however, as the berries are soft and will make a mess if they are allowed to drop. Also fruiting at this season are the many different pyracanthas. These will grow and produce their masses of berries quite cheerfully on a north wall or in the open, thriving in any soil and equally happy in sun or shade. These shrubs are evergreen and they have a long period of usefulness to the flower arranger with blossom in June and berries lasting throughout the winter, if the birds leave them alone – they are said to be less interested in the *P. atalantioides* than in other species.

Some roses last on into the autumn, ramblers like Zephirine Drouhin or pillar roses like Dance du Feu and Golden Showers. These roses are easier to manage than the highly bred standards and with a little cutting out and dead-heading will produce a most satisfying succession of flowers until the frost ends their season. There are also varieties of roses that are truly shrubby they are listed as Bourbon roses, Cabbage roses, Moss roses, etc., many of these are valued for fruit or fragrant foliage as well as for the blossom. One of the China roses – Cecile Brunner – produces tiny pink roses from late May until October and may be considered a rose for a small garden as the bush grows no higher than three feet and is about the same through. Some of these hardy souls do give lovely blossom for the flower arranger and it is amazing how long they will continue to bloom.

WINTER

Many spring flowering shrubs may yield a few flowers in the late winter if the weather is mild but to be sure of blossom in the winter months it is best to obtain those which may be relied upon to bloom in December, January and February.

Some berried shrubs will retain their fruit through the winter but there are also both shrubs and perennials that bloom in the most gloomy parts of the year. Many of these have pale flowers – the racemes of the *Garrya elliptica* and some of the hellebores for example – but these delicate colours are particularly suitable for winter arrangements and emphasize the short days of winter broken by odd gleams of sunshine.

The winter jasmine is widely grown and well known to us all. This is a surety for flower no matter what the weather – a few branches cut and brought indoors will soon produce the gay little flowers along the bare green branches. Many of these early (or should it be late?) flowers produce their blossom before the foliage and evergreen foliage or preserved foliage must be found to complete the arrangement. The flowers of the Chimonanthus (Winter Sweet) are pale primrose and come out in the middle of the winter, like many other inconspicuous flowers of this period, they would probably be overlooked if they were in competition with the gay flowers of spring and summer. The beauty of the *Iris Stylosa*, for example, is in the contrast of its delicacy with the harsh days of its flowering season.

Forced flowers of all kinds can be found in the winter, of course, but for the student of Ikebana they do not have the same appeal or significance as have the true flowers of the season. *Viburnum fragrans* is a very hardy shrub and can be depended on for flowers from December onwards and so can the supposedly autumn flowering prunus (*P. subhirtella autumnalis*), picked in bud this prunus will flower when brought into the warmth of the house and a few warm days will see the tree in blossom in the garden. The Cornelian Cherry (*Cornus Mas*) will flower on bare wood in February, the flowers are yellow and very good for cutting.

As with most of the flowering shrubs the bushes will need time, after planting, to become established before much demand can be made upon them for arrangements but the amount of blossom will increase as the plant settles into its position. One shrub which will provide both flower and foliage at this difficult season is the Mahonia japonica which has bold evergreen leaves and long spikes of pale lemon, lily-of-the-valley perfumed flowers. A sheltered position will be appreciated and will help to bring the flowers out early – I know of at least one mahonia that is in bloom in November, due to its protected situation, although my own will not usually bloom until December.

One of the most attractive sights to be found in a winter bound garden is a patch of the hardy miniature cyclamen. A number of different species may be planted beneath trees or shrubs to provide flowers throughout the year but they are most welcome in winter. The varieties *Cyclamen coum* and *C. vernum* will last

through the winter months and, when the plants are
well established, will provide a large number of flowers.
The leaves are as attractive as the flowers and, as they
are shorter in the stem, they form a dark green ' mat '
beneath the delicate petals. Cyclamens last well in arrangements and the corms become increasingly free
flowering if they are left undisturbed.

The *Iris stylosa* is another of these delicate-looking
hardy plants. *Iris unguicularis* is the correct botanical
name but many gardeners know it as *Iris stylosa* and
love it for its double attraction of orchid-like flowers
and hardy nature. A few mild days will see a new crop
of buds, picked at this stage they will open and last
well in the house; the stems are a little on the short
side but this presents no difficulty to the follower of
Ikebana. I know of a large clump of *Iris stylosa* on the
south side of a low wall in very poor ground which
flowers most cheerfully through the worst of the winter.
Again, these plants take a little while to settle but once
established in a well drained, sunny position where the
soil is not too rich they will flower freely. Do not disturb
this iris unless absolutely necessary and even then do
not divide it into too many pieces as it will take a long
time to recover.

Bergenias are well known to flower arrangers both
for leaf and blossom. They are usually reckoned to be
spring flowers but given reasonable shelter under shrubs
or in woodland the panicles of pink blossom will begin
to appear in December.

Hellebores – the Christmas Rose is only one of a
large family – are worth a little investigation. It is

not always easy to find the position most to their liking but, when successful, your efforts will be greatly rewarded in the dreary winter days. Shelter from the wind, partial shade and moist but well-drained soil should fill the requirements of these plants. Positions in woodland and around shrubs are suitable and convenient too, because most of the hellebores make attractive ground cover; mulching with peat or leaf mould will help to reserve moisture and care should be taken to disturb the plants as little as possible. The flowers last for a long period in the garden and will do well indoors providing they are given a good drink with the whole stem, previously split for an inch or so of its length, in deep water.

Pyracanthas are evergreen and hardy and the berries of many of them will last all through the winter as will those of the *Skimmia japonica*. This latter shrub does not grow over large but unless the *S. foremanii,* which produces both male and female flowers, is grown it will be necessary to have a male bush to ensure pollination.

Camellias give rich green foliage in the winter and can be combined with hellebores to the advantage of both. Ivy, with its wide variety of species, is evergreen and some of the decorative ones can be trained into small bushes or used to cover an old tree stump; the twisted leafy branches are useful at any time of the year. Make use also of interestingly shaped bare branches and contrasting feathery fronds of the chamaecyparis for winter arrangements. Some shrubs have distinctively coloured shoots in the days between the leaf fall and the new growth in the spring – *Leycesteria formosa* for green, and cornus varieties for red and yellow . These will add welcome colour to an arrangement where dried or preserved material is mainly used.

The following rule of the Sogetsu School of Ikebana holds good for both your gardening and your flower arrangements :

'Train your eyes to grow appreciative and your hands to become creative, and make constant efforts to improve your skill.'

To it I would add one of my own :

'Enjoy yourself.'

INDEX